T0161213

JAPANESE THROWING WEAPONS

Mastering Shuriken Throwing Techniques

DANIEL FLETCHER

Foreword by **Yasuyuki Otsuka**

TUTTLE Publishing

Tokyo | Rutland, Vermont | Singapore

ABOUT TUTTLE
"Books to Span the East and West"

Our core mission at Tuttle Publishing is to create books which bring people together one page at a time. Tuttle was founded in 1832 in the small New England town of Rutland, Vermont (USA). Our fundamental values remain as strong today as they were then—to publish best-in-class books informing the English-speaking world about the countries and peoples of Asia. The world has become a smaller place today and Asia's economic, cultural and political influence has expanded, yet the need for meaningful dialogue and information about this diverse region has never been greater. Since 1948, Tuttle has been a leader in publishing books on the cultures, arts, cuisines, languages and literatures of Asia. Our authors and photographers have won numerous awards and Tuttle has published thousands of books on subjects ranging from martial arts to paper crafts. We welcome you to explore the wealth of information available on Asia at www.tuttlepublishing.com.

Published by Tuttle Publishing, an imprint of Periplus Editions (HK) Ltd.

www.tuttlepublishing.com

Copyright © 2011 Daniel Fletcher

Library of Congress Cataloging-in-Publication Data
ISBN 978-4-8053-1101-1

Fletcher, Danny.
Japanese throwing weapons: mastering shuriken throwing techniques / Danny Fletcher; foreword by Yasuyuki Otsuka Sensei.
   p. cm.
  ISBN 978-4-8053-1101-1 (pbk.)
1. Martial arts weapons--Japan. 2. Weapons--Japan. 3. Knife throwing. I. Title.
GV1101.5.F54 2011
796.8--dc22

2010037349

Distributed by

North America, Latin America & Europe
Tuttle Publishing, 364 Innovation Drive
North Clarendon, VT 05759-9436 U.S.A.
Tel: 1 (802) 773-8930
Fax: 1 (802) 773-6993
info@tuttlepublishing.com
www.tuttlepublishing.com

Japan
Tuttle Publishing, Yaekari Building,
3rd Floor, 5-4-12 Osaki, Shinagawa-ku
Tokyo 141 0032
Tel: (81) 3 5437-0171
Fax: (81) 3 5437-0755
sales@tuttle.co.jp
www.tuttle.co.jp

Asia Pacific
Berkeley Books Pte. Ltd.
3 Kallang Sector #04-01
Singapore 349278
Tel: (65) 6741-2178
Fax: (65) 67414-2179
inquiries@periplus.com.sg
www.periplus.com

First edition
23 22 21 20 19   1903CM
10 9 8 7 6 5 4

Printed in China

Contents

Foreword 5

Shuriken-jutsu 8

Bo Shuriken 23

Throwing Basics 26

Advanced Meifu Shinkage Ryu Shuriken-jutsu: The Jissen Kata . . . 44

Uchibari 47

Chishin Ryu 50

Shirai Ryu 52

Nage-ya Shuriken 54

Negishi Ryu 57

Shaken 60

Juji Shaken 64

Togakure Ryu Senban 67

Teppan 74

Kunai 77

Tsugawa Ryu 79

Iga Ryu 81

Combat Techniques 83

Insights 108

Training, Targets and Safety 116

The Meifu Shinkage Ryu Research Group 122

Acknowledgments 128

Foreword

In this book, you will be receiving valuable instructions on the Japanese martial art of shuriken-jutsu. The author, Danny Fletcher, is my student and has studied shuriken-jutsu directly under me in Japan. I have been teaching and guiding students of shuriken-jutsu for about 25 years. It was fortunate for him that I had a web site for the Meifu-Shinkage Ryu since 1999. In May 2004, he sent me an e-mail and came to Tokyo from Funabashi to meet me.

Danny said to me that he had lived in Japan several years, and was studying another martial art already. In addition to his learning other martial arts, he was hoping to master Japanese shuriken-jutsu. So, I explained to him about Meifu Shinkage Ryu shuriken-jutsu. In addition to speaking with him, I demonstrated our shuriken-jutsu methods. It seemed that my demonstration impressed him, because that same day he became one of my students.

After entering Meifu Shinkage Ryu, he trained diligently at every class. To my surprise, he was very familiar with Japanese martial arts. He has considerable knowledge about ken-jutsu, ju-jutsu, and other arts. He said he was really surprised to see someone throw a shuriken at such long distances or throw them so fast.

Even here in Japan, there are very few people who have knowledge of shuriken-jutsu. In Japan, the birthplace of shuriken-jutsu, there are few teachers of shuriken-jutsu who can teach their students properly. There are probably fewer than five such men.

My teacher, Mr. Chikatoshi Someya, was the founder of the Meifu Shinkage Ryu. Someya Sensei was a master of Katori Shinto Ryu. Katori Shinto Ryu is a classical Japanese martial art (Ko-budo). After studying for many years, he established his own school that teaches shuriken-jutsu. This was in the 1960's and he named his school the Meifu Shinkage Ryu. (MSR)

He wrote a book about his studies of shuriken-jutsu, and opened a dojo to the public. It was a revolutionary event in Japanese antique budo (martial arts). Classical martial artists don't usually offer to teach their techniques to the public, especially shuriken-jutsu, which was considered a secret weapon for hundreds of years. So, there is very little research material about shuriken-jutsu in Japan. This is also the reason why there are so very few shuriken-jutsu teachers. Someya Sensei was very disappointed with those circumstances. He was afraid that the art of shuriken-jutsu might die and become a forgotten part of Japanese history. Therefore, he taught the previously secret shuriken-jutsu to the public.

I joined his shuriken school in 1984 after reading his book. After joining the Meifu Shinkage Ryu, I practiced earnestly and became a master after ten years. To my regret, Someya Sensei passed away in 1999, but I was appointed his successor during his lifetime. I succeeded my teacher's instruction, and decided to continue to pursue his dream of preserving this art.

I set up my web site on the Internet and began sending information about shuriken-jutsu to not only Japan, but also the world. In 2004, I published a book and a DVD. As time went on, my efforts began to pay off, there were many people sending me e-mails from a dozen different countries. Some of them visited me and became my students. Danny Fletcher was one of them.

Danny is a very large man from a Japanese point of view. When I compared the size of my hands with his, I suggested that he use an extra-long shuriken. He is large, but the principles of shuriken-jutsu don't change. I treated him the same way as any Japanese student except for the size of his shuriken. Now, he uses regular-sized shuriken.

Meifu Shinkage Ryu at Katori Shrine in Japan

Of course, our linguistic differences sometimes caused a little difficulty in teaching, but it was not a big problem for us. Shuriken-jutsu can't be explained just in words. If you learn old Japanese martial arts, you must observe your teacher's movement.

Danny observed my shuriken-jutsu very carefully and understood the meaning. After about three years of training with me, he acquired his sho-dan (black belt). He understands the essence of shuriken-jutsu. Now, he is back in his home in Texas, and has completed this book. This is the result of Danny's hard training in Japan. Anyone who has an interest in the ancient Japanese martial arts should read this book.

There is something important I want to share with you. My teacher, Someya Sensei, gave this to me. All students of the Meifu Shinkage Ryu should understand this admonition:

You must not become attached to the idea of piercing the target.
If you do, you may desire more targets to pierce.
The heart that desires a target is the same as the heart that desires
    an enemy.

Desiring an enemy is foolishness.
Foolishness is the darkness of your heart.

If you live sincerely, your heart will hold no shadows.
If your heart and deeds are pure, then you will never encounter an
    enemy.
Then, time and distance are transcended and you will defeat any
    enemy.
This is "Shin-da." (Truly pierced.)

Yasuyuki Otsuka.
Headmaster of Meifu Shinkage Ryu.
2011

(See page 115 for original Japanese text of this creed.)

Shuriken-jutsu

For nearly a thousand years, there have been schools in Japan dedicated to the art of killing. The ancient schools of martial arts instructed students in every facet of survival in a hostile environment, including castle design, first aid, stress management, and more. The martial arts we see so often these days bear only a vague resemblance to their true origins. There is nothing wrong with using parts of budo in order to teach virtues, morals and physical fitness, but there are much more serious kinds of teachings that exist in the ancient *densho* (written records) and *kuden* (personal transmissions) of the original schools. Most people have no idea of the serious nature of real budo. While it is perfectly understandable that your average parent would not want his or her child actually learning how to kill, it must be understood that these arts were not created for the purpose of entertainment or for sport or for self-improvement—they certainly were not intended for children. The martial arts were intended to train soldiers in how to do their jobs, just as modern militaries train their recruits in the use of the rifle, bayonet, and grenade. The purpose of this book is to introduce you to the teachings of only one small piece of that life-and-death world of budo.

The word shuriken (shoo-ree-ken: The Japanese "r" sounds like a soft "d") is a Japanese term for small pieces of metal used as throwing weapons. They appear quite often in films and on TV, so it's unlikely that anyone would not recognize their basic form and function, even if it's only at a superficial level.

This is a selection of different types of shuriken.

Shuriken-jutsu means "hand release blade techniques." It entails using shuriken in combat, primarily by throwing, but also by cutting or thrusting. For a long time, the practice of throwing shuriken has been most commonly associated with the ninja, but they were not the only users of these weapons. In fact, every Japanese school of martial arts has had, at some point in its history, at least one form of shuriken-jutsu in their teachings.

As a matter of fact, these weapons are not entirely unknown in the west. During the First World War, similar weapons were used as "bomblets" dropped by the hundreds from aircraft over enemy troops.

In World War I the Germans used these air darts.

It is thought that some of the earliest Japanese practices of shuriken-jutsu were examples of warriors throwing their short swords in battle. The samurai carried two or three swords: a long sword, a short sword and a dagger. The odds of striking a fatal blow against an armored opponent by throwing a short sword are very low. It was an unlikely maneuver, but not totally without merit, as practice in throwing the short sword became common. In some cases, even the long sword was thrown.

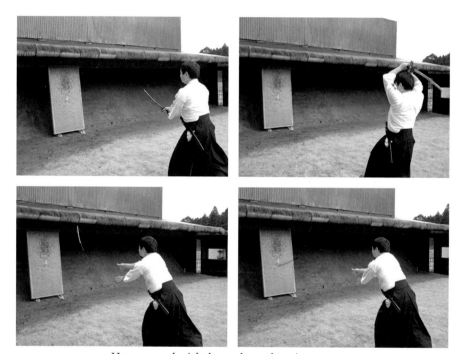

How a sword might be used as a throwing weapon.

The shuriken was never a weapon of great strategic importance to an army on the battlefield. During the Warring States period (1450 to 1600 AD), as in many other countries, battles were fought by large, strategically directed formations of men using weapons of distance.

When thousands of men joined in combat, weapons of range made the strategic difference. Long-distance weapons (cannon, firearms and the bow) were the great killers in feudal Japan (along with deliberately set fires). Formations fired on enemy formations; so combat was not typically man-to-man. Cannons would start the battle and then muskets and bows were employed. The ability to kill at a distance is the secret to survival in war.

Cavalry and long spear formations would move around and basically finish the battle. Some of those spears were as long as 18 feet. Even though the spear was a hand-held weapon, it still provided the advantage of killing at a distance.

For those who were lucky enough to carry them, the firearm was the undisputed supreme weapon. It had the range and power to kill that far exceeded the bow. The bow, however, was the main weapon before the arrival of firearms and continued to be used in great numbers even after the matchlock rifle appeared in battle. Once the sides closed and the advantage of the gun or bow was lost, armies fought with long spears. However, if a soldier lost his spear, he was in trouble, now he no longer had the ability to strike from a distance.

There are many pole arms that provide some distance, but in facing a line of thousands of long spears, only another long spear will be of use. There is a point, however, where an enemy gets too close for even a spear to be useful. There are a number of situations where an enemy can reach you before you can reload your musket or nock another arrow. This distance is the traditional domain of the sword, but it is also the domain of the shuriken.

One could say the shuriken was of great importance to an individual soldier on the battlefield, especially if he were to find himself on the losing side. Once the battle was clearly decided, the losers had three choices: be killed, be captured or escape. At this point, the possibility for close-quarters single combat was a distinct possibility. As the distance between combatants closed and their options ran out, the losing side had no choice but to resort to individual, last-ditch techniques. Such circumstances give rise to an artistic level of survival-inspired creativity. A soldier could find many possible weapons in the litter of a fresh battlefield—weapons lying on the ground or protruding from bodies like broken spears, broken swords, discarded knives, thousands of broken arrows, and pieces of broken armor plate. This may be why Tatsumi Ryu shuriken bear a very strong resemblance to a traditional Japanese yari (spear head).

Tatsumi Ryu Shuriken

Any of these battlefield remnants could be used as a *buki* (weapon) or as *me-tsubushi* (blinder/distraction). As a soldier on the losing side, all you had to do to survive was get off the field of battle and run. Even if you did not manage to kill your attackers, a distraction, a chance to escape would be enough. The chances of survival are much greater for the man who decides to distract his enemy and escape than for the man who decides to engage in combat.

After the age of wars there came a time of peace known as the Edo period (1600 to 1868 AD). The Edo period is called a peaceful period because there were no more great battles and widespread warring, but that does not mean that individuals were no longer fighting and killing other individuals with regularity. Many of the existing schools of martial arts were founded during the early Edo period. Often these schools "tested" each other by dueling, sometimes to the death, for the honor of their school. The early Edo period also saw thousands and thousands of suddenly unemployed soldiers roaming the countryside who had no other means of making a living. No longer were the fighting men confined to battlefields. During this time of "peace," the potential for violence to individuals was possibly higher than during the age of wars. Crime was everywhere and there were few police officers. During the early Edo period, the Japanese people started to rebuild their country and grew wealthy, but violence and the fear of violence never left them. The practice of carrying (and using) concealed weapons became commonplace with men and women. There is a story from this period of the famous swordsman Musashi throwing his sword at an opponent. Musashi was losing a duel and was facing death. Were it not for shuriken-jutsu, the man reputed to be "the world's greatest swordsman" would have been killed by a master of the *kusarigama* (chain and sickle). He was not the first or last warrior to do this.

Even today, training in shuriken-jutsu is tied closely to the use of the sword. Shuriken are usually thrown before or during the drawing of the sword or they are thrown during a sword fight as a surprise attack. There are even some shuriken designed to be held between the hand and the sword itself, making it easy to use both at the same time. Some martial arts schools consider the *kozuka* (by-knife) that is carried in the *saya* (scabbard) of the katana to be their only type of shuriken.

The *kozuka* was a small knife attached to the scabbard of the sword.

During the Warring States period and Edo periods, an incredible amount of creativity occurred with regard to weapons design and methods of concealing them. Every conceivable form of hand-held weapon found use in Japan at this time. Smaller, more concealable weapons, like the shuriken, were exploited and employed to a great extent. New schools were created and new shuriken designs and methods of hiding them on the body were developed.

Meifu Shinkage Ryu

The Meifu Shinkage Ryu is primarily a bo shuriken school. As such, we will only be discussing in depth the bo shuriken throw. There are two throwing techniques: the basic throw and the advanced throw. The basic throw will enable you to throw the shuriken and stick it in the target reliably and accurately. Compared to the advanced throw it is relatively slow and obvious, but without mastering the basic throw the advanced throw is impossible to learn. The advanced throw also contains a few secrets that Otsuka Sensei wishes to reserve only for his actual students and will not be discussed in this book. (Although there are some hints!) This is the way of many schools and is meant to encourage you to go to Japan and learn in person. Martial arts are not sterile, impersonal sets of factual information. They are living things that are passed down from teacher to student and they remain so to this day.

The Meifu Shinkage Ryu is a small school of martial arts in Tokyo, Japan. They are relatively unknown in the martial arts world and have fewer than forty students. There are no dojos or teachers outside of Japan and there is only one dojo in Tokyo. That "dojo" exists only in rented spaces for a few hours a week. The school is growing, however. Recently a small dojo was opened in Osaka and there are now two *keikokai* (informal training groups) outside of Japan. The reason behind its growth is the amazing skill of the present headmaster, Yasuykui Otsuka. His ability to throw shuriken with uncanny speed, accuracy and distance is far beyond that of any other masters of the art.

The Meifu Shinkage Ryu school was founded by the late Chikatoshi Someya. (1923–1999) When he was younger, Someya Sensei was a student of the Sugino branch of the Katori Shinto Ryu, a famous sword school. He was always very interested in shuriken-jutsu. In his later years, he decided to form his own

Someya Sensei

school that focused solely on the shuriken. He maintained a good relationship with his former colleagues and to this day the Sugino Katori Shinto Ryu has a strong tie to the Meifu Shinkage Ryu. He devoted himself to refining and perfecting the art of shuriken-jutsu and some other concealed weapons.

At one time, there were several teachers of the Meifu Shinkage Ryu, but old age and illness have dwindled their number down to one. Otsuka Sensei believes that this number is going to rise very rapidly in the near future,

The Meifu Shinkage Ryu training focuses primarily on throwing the shuriken, but they also teach some hand-to-hand shuriken techniques, sword, chain and some unusual concealed weapons, such as the *sho-ken* (a small stabbing weapon).

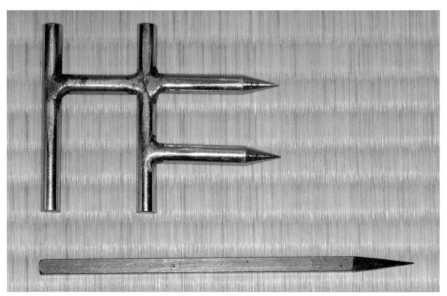

Examples of the *sho-ken* (above left) and bo shuriken (below right).

Someya Sensei developed a fast and powerful throw, a technique that is limited in body movement, making it hard to see. To complement this new technique, he modified the design of his shuriken. He experimented with shuriken from different schools, and he also made and tested many new designs, searching for the perfect size and shape for his refined technique. He decided on the design the Meifu Shinkage Ryu uses today.

Shuriken prototypes developed by the Meifu Shinkage Ryu.

The original Katori Shinto Ryu blades owned by Someya Sensei resemble a type of bo shuriken called *uchibari* (house needles). These shuriken are common to many budo schools in Japan, including the Kukishinden Ryu and the Togakure Ryu. Not all shuriken called *uchibari* are identical. The "square torpedo" shape can be seen in several examples, often varying greatly in size.

These are examples of antique *uchibari.*

Otsuka Sensei likes to refer to the school as a "research group." He uses this term because the study of the school is not wholly limited to the use of Meifu Shinkage Ryu weapons. He enjoys practicing with shuriken from many different schools (most of which are now extinct.) Almost all of the students in the Meifu Shinkage Ryu are students of other martial arts schools. Training is somewhat informal and open-minded when compared to other traditional Japanese schools of the martial arts.

Just as a modern police officer may carry a shotgun in his car, a service pistol on his belt, a backup pistol on his ankle, a baton, pepper spray, a taser and a knife, so too did ancient warriors carry an assortment of weapons, some were concealed and some were not. Samurai were allowed to carry any size and number of weapons they wanted, but they also carried shuriken secreted on their persons. A person of lesser status or a spy (ninja) would probably not wear any weapons openly but might have more than a dozen shuriken hidden in his clothing.

The people who lived through those dangerous times left behind an amazing diversity of weapons in form and function that is reminiscent of the innumerable species of insects you might see in a museum. Nowhere is this more evident than shuriken. In general, there are three categories of shuriken:

- **Bo shuriken:** "stick-like blades"
- *Shaken* **shuriken:** "wheel blades" Also called *Hira* shuriken "flat blade" or *Senban* shuriken "lathe blade."
- *Teppan* **shuriken:** "iron plate blade"

In this book we will be looking at all three major categories of shuriken. We will discuss the different types, how they are thrown and how they were used as hand-held weapons. It is a gross overstatement and a mistake to suggest that one group of military men used any one type of shuriken exclusively, however, for the sake of clarity and maximizing the educational benefit of this book, we are going to divide the shuriken between two main schools (despite the fact that both schools use shuriken from both groups). There will be overlap, but that is a good thing. Our two schools will be the Meifu Shinkage Ryu and the Bujinkan (which is actually nine old budo schools taught together). We will look at the bo shuriken-jutsu of the Meifu Shinkage Ryu and the *senban* and *teppan* use of the Bujinkan.

Bo shuriken, as the name suggests, are stick-like (straight). They take many forms and sizes and most of them are between long 4 to 7 inches (12 and 18 cm) and weigh 1 ounce to 6 ounces (30 to 180 grams). In cross-section, they may be round, triangular, square, hexagonal or octagonal. They may be of constant thickness or they may taper sharply. Their shape usually depends upon their origin. Some shuriken designs evolved from common objects. Bo shuriken are often descended from nails, nail-drivers (*kugi-oshi*), metal chopsticks used to tend coals, broken arrowheads, broken spear heads, broken sword tips, unmounted knife blades, hair ornaments, by-knives, large needles, etc. Sometimes, however, they are original designs intended only for combat. The bo shuriken is by far the most commonly used type of shuriken in Japanese martial arts, perhaps because of the universal shape

Bo shuriken can come in a variety of shapes and sizes.

of its design. There are two major categories of bo shuriken: rod-like and dart-like. Rods are plain pieces of straight metal (non-aerodynamic). Darts are aerodynamic and have tails incorporated into their designs. The distinction is entirely subjective, but will help in understanding why the throwing methods differ between these two types.

Here are examples of bo and *teppan* shuriken.

Shaken **shuriken** are basically star-shaped, flat pieces of metal. *Shaken* means wheel-shaped-blade. They can have any number of points of varying shape. (Just as any modern craftsman would have many different kinds of drill bits, for example). They tend to be 4 to 6 inches (10cm to 15cm) tip to tip, and .03 inches to .23 inches (1mm to 6mm) thick, but most are less than 2mm.The word *senban*, in Japanese, means a woodcutting lathe. That suggests that many *senban* blades were originally cutting tools used to shape wood by Japan's pre-modern craftsmen. Some *senban* are intended to be used with a sword, some are meant to be used on their own. Some examples may have been used as washers or brackets in architecture. One well-known *senban* blade was a tool for removing nails.

One could argue that each individual design deserves its own classification, but this book is not an attempt to historically classify and define all shuriken with Linnaean taxonomy. The aim of this book is to help the student become proficient in throwing shuriken with the correct, authentic techniques as taught in Japan. For this reason, I have decided to refer to all shuriken of this type as *shaken* and divided them into two main categories: piercing and cutting blades. The reason for this distinction is found in the tendency to hold and employ them differently. Knowing the exact name for each blade is not necessary; only understanding the nature of the blade is important.

This is a display of various *senban* shuriken.

The concept of *shaken* shuriken has a long history reaching back to China and India. The chakram of ancient India is undoubtedly an ancestor of the modern Japanese weapon. The routes to Japan can be traced and delineated by the migrating cultural traditions that bore them. Mountain ascetics brought some *shaken* to Japan from China, most of the others were of indigenous origin.

It is not difficult to imagine the ordinary beginnings for many of them. Possible local sources for these weapons can still be seen today in Japanese antique shops and in the architecture of shrines and temples. One may see metal brackets in shrines that, if pulled from their mountings, would be instantly usable as throwing weapons. These are large brass or iron washers held in place by large iron nails, which, interestingly enough, are also very similar in size and shape to some bo shuriken.

Samples of brackets from shrines that could have been used as weapons.

Not all shuriken were quotidian items, some were intentionally manu-factured as weapons—more than likely there was a mixture of both.

The *shaken* is particularly well known. It has become the symbol of the ninja in Japan, but that is only a modern association. The ninja did use them, no doubt, but so did the other military men of the time.

Teppan shuriken include several different designs that are flat, like *shaken*, but are not necessarily star-shaped. *Teppan* means a flat, metal plate. *Shaken* are a kind of *teppan*, but not all *teppan* are *shaken*. There are not many of these designs, but what examples do exist are well known, such as the Tsugawa Ryu blades and the Iga Ryu blades. Both of these weapons were used as tools in carpentry, architecture, pottery and agriculture. Similar tools are still available in Japan.

Tsugawa Ryu Blade

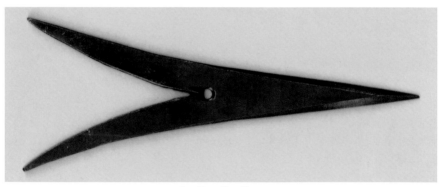

Iga Ryu Shuriken

It is interesting to note that the Iga Ryu shuriken bears a resemblance to the V-shaped bracket seen in the upper right of the photo on page 24. I do not believe they are related, seeing that the Iga Ryu blade has a fairly certain origin as a carpenter's tool, but someone who knew shuriken-jutsu would recognize such objects almost everywhere and would be able to employ those similar objects if needed.

This is an important thing to remember about shuriken-jutsu: The actual blades are weapons, but the skill itself gives the practitioner the ability to employ any object of similar size and shape. If you knew you were going to be searched, then you wouldn't take your blades with you. You would already know that you could acquire blades by scavenging a shrine or wood shop or any other place where such tools and hardware would be found.

Bo Shuriken

Because the ancient schools often borrowed and shared weapons and techniques, it may not be possible to definitively classify every specimen by school. The bo shuriken can be found in uncounted variations. A good example of this variety would be the *uchibari*. There are two main examples: a thin blade and a fat blade. Modern Katori Shinto Ryu practitioners tend to believe that the "fat" *uchibari* is the true Katori Shinto Ryu blade. Someya Sensei passed down a collection of his own Katori Shinto Ryu blades that are "thin." The blades attributed to the Kukishinden Ryu and Togakure Ryu are also what we could call "thin" blades. It may be that the Katori Shinto Ryu blades were not actually *uchibari*, but simply a different blade of similar shape but of larger size and differing origin. The thin blades may have been nails while the fat blades were the nail-drivers. There are also regional differences in tools and weapons throughout Japan. Some regions use a very long-bladed axe while some use a short bladed axe, but all for the same purpose. Schools, regions, makers, and time periods all affect the morphology of shuriken.

This kind of similarity between shuriken of different schools is quite common, but should not be of any real concern.

Some people may argue that certain morphologies are definitive and their labels are unequivocal, but it would be foolish to assume that students of one school never used the blades associated with another. (Often two schools descended from a common ancestor.)

Some weapons were unique, but for the most part, they were diverse and wide-ranging. If two shuriken are identical but their owners claim they are unique, then so be it. Shuriken are, after all, just pieces of metal, and unlike insects, have no DNA to be tested.

The Katori Shinto Ryu blade (above) compared to an *uchibari*.

You can see how antique Japanese nails or *kugi* (on the left) and antique nail driver or *kugi-oshi* (on the right) could be used as throwing weapons.

The standard Meifu Shinkage Ryu shuriken is 15cm long, 6mm thick, of square cross-section, and weighs about 40 grams. The 25mm points are hardened, but the body metal is soft. This is true of all shuriken—they are not like knives made of quality, hardened steel.

Meifu Shinkage Ryu Blades

A shuriken needs to sit in the hand a certain way. Since human hands vary in size and flexibility, the length and thickness of the shuriken can be adjusted. The size of shuriken used in the Meifu Shinkage Ryu dojo ranges from 5 to 6 inches (14 to 17 cm) in length, and from .2 to .3 inches (5 to 8 mm) in thickness. The total weight of the shuriken is important. The advanced Meifu Shinkage Ryu throw requires a snap of the wrist. Trying to snap the wrist while throwing a 5.5 ounce (150 grams) shuriken will usually end in failure and injury to the wrist. The design of the Meifu Shinkage Ryu shuriken is very simple. It resembles, in size and shape, pencils, pens and many other common objects a person is likely to carry. It is easy to manufacture and requires no blacksmithing, which also makes it inexpensive.

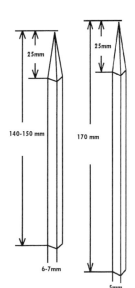

Some of the differences in size for shuriken.

Throwing Basics

There are two basic ways to use the shuriken:

Daken-jutsu 打剣術 Throwing techniques
Shoken-jutsu 掌剣術 Hand-to-hand techniques

These methods are really two possible outcomes of the same exact circumstance: A blade (or any object) is hidden in the hand of a person who must defend himself from an armed attacker. This is an important concept in our training. When we practice, we try to cultivate a sense of preparedness for any use, not just throwing.

Daken-jutsu 打剣術 Throwing Techniques

A shuriken can be any object, it does not have to be a blade. It could be a pencil, chopstick, paintbrush or a tool. The shuriken may be thrown without preparation or hesitation. In this respect, it is faster than the bow and arrow, the sword or even the gun. A shuriken can allow you to hit an enemy who is too far away for punching or kicking. There is an effective limit to this ability, however, which is usually ten meters. In budo, distance is measured in *ken*, which is equal to the length of one tatami mat or the distance the average swordsman can reach with his sword held out at arm's length, approximately 70 inches (180 cm).

The length of your throw is determined by measuring the distance between your front foot and the target at the time of the release. In the old budo schools, the practiced limit for shuriken-jutsu was three tatami mats' length. (*sangen* 三間) which is about 17 feet (5.4 meters). In a real fight, this is not much distance. It is a good idea to be able to throw from slightly further distances, such as 22 feet (7.2 meters) (*yongen* 四間) and 29 feet (9 meters) (*goken* 五間).

When a human throws an object, his arm moves in a circle. The arm is a line that is stationary at one end, the shoulder, and may move freely from there. Punching tends to be a straight, extending movement. Punching can generate a lot of power, but throwing generates great speed. Throwing a shuriken is not done by extending the arm towards the target. Shuriken are thrown by moving the arm in a circular motion, much like throwing a baseball. Because the arm rotates during the throwing motion, the object that is being thrown will also rotate. The art of shuriken-jutsu is the art of controlling the rate at which thrown objects will rotate as they fly through the air.

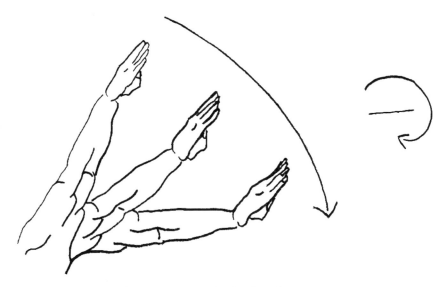

The arm rotates, so the shuriken also rotates.

Shuriken, like all other missiles, are subject to gravity and exhibit a parabolic flight path. If one were to simply "push" the shuriken straight at the target, it would simply bounce off, having turned in flight because of low speed, gravity and uncontrolled rotation. The success of the throw depends upon your ability to control the velocity and speed of rotation. Once you master this concept, you will become able to throw almost any linear object with success.

There are three ways to throw the bo shuriken:

1. *Jikidaho* 直打法 (direct hit)
2. *Hantendaho* 反転打法 (reverse hit)
3. *Takaitendaho* 多回転打法 (fast spinning, like knife throwing)

Japanese schools employ *jikidaho* or *hantendaho* for bo shuriken and *takaitendaho* for *shaken* shuriken.

Jikidaho 直打法 Direct Hit Throwing

Jikidaho is the direct hit method of throwing. This means that the shuriken is held with the tip pointing out, away from the palm. When you throw the shuriken, it leaves your hand with its point in the air and its tail towards the ground. As it flies, it turns slowly, so that the shuriken is horizontal just before it strikes the target.

The *jikidaho* grip: The shuriken lies between the first and second fingers. The thumb presses the shuriken against the base of the third finger. The butt of the shuriken rests against the palm near the base of the thumb. (Above that upside-down "Y.") This is one of the reasons that bo shuriken of square cross-section are so much easier to throw than other designs. The facets of the blade cause it to fit perfectly in the gap between your first and second fingers. It also keeps the shuriken from sliding around during the throw and provides two flat surfaces for your fingers to brush during the release. The *jikidaho* method is the basis for many other throws, so it is important to master it.

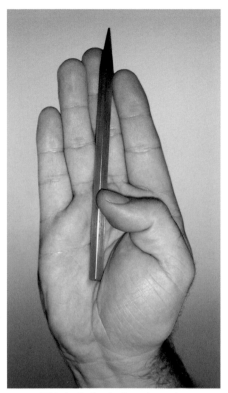

This is the basic throwing grip.

The shuriken is released and it turns 90 degrees as it flies. This is a basic idea common to many shuriken schools. The Meifu Shinkage Ryu, however, employs a pushing with the palm against the base of the shuriken in its throw. Not only that, but the arm is flexed up and down and the wrist is snapped. This refined technique gives the shuriken a very fast, flat trajectory. The Meifu Shinkage Ryu shuriken is smaller than most: the size and shape were developed to take ad-vantage of the school's unique palm-pushing method.

Hantendaho 反転打法 Reverse Hit Throwing

If you change the direction of the shuriken in your hand so that the point is touching your palm, this is the "*hantendaho* grip." The shuriken, when thrown, will turn 180 degrees in the air before striking the target. This technique does not employ high-speed throwing techniques like the *jikidaho* throw. (No pushing with the palm, obviously, as you would impale yourself on the shuriken) The feeling of this throw is very similar to that of the curveball in baseball.

Hantendaho is really just for practice in the Meifu Shinkage Ryu; it is a good way for beginners to enjoy throwing at a target from longer distances until they have mastered the *jikidaho* throw. It is also used for combat throwing with the heavier blades in other schools, like the Chishin Ryu.

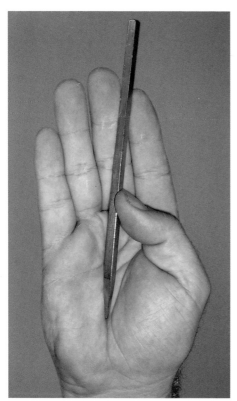

This is the reverse grip with the point in the palm.

Throwing Practice

Before you begin throwing, make sure that you have a matching set of clean, sharp blades. They should all be the exact same type, length, and weight. Try not to make too much noise when picking them up or putting them down. If you must speak while people are training, do so in a quiet voice. You do not want to distract someone who is throwing a live weapon in close proximity. Always use common sense.

Similar to some other martial arts, the practice of shuriken-jutsu begins from a natural, peaceful state. Try to cultivate a sense of calmness and serenity. This is the beginning, the *kamae* (attitude) of patience and non-hostility. When walking and standing, the shuriken are carried, point-down, in the dominant hand or tucked into the obi. This is done for safety. The shuriken are in your dominant hand, but you keep them and your intentions secret.

This is how to carry the blades.

This is how the blades are typically worn in the obi.

Once you approach the target and are ready to begin, make sure you are holding the blades correctly, while in a natural stance (*shizentai*). With the back straight and with both hands curled in a light fist on the sides of the hips, face forward (towards the target) and quietly bow.

This is the stance before beginning (*kamae*).   Take a half step and transfer the shuriken.

Upon completing the bow, lightly take one step forward, transferring the blades from the throwing hand to the other hand. Do this very slowly and carefully. The shuriken should still be point-down.

With the shuriken in the left hand, extend the left arm towards the target. The left arm should be pointing straight towards the target and the right hand should be resting on the right hip.

How the shuriken are held in the left hand.

Left arm is extended toward the target.

Bring the first blade to the right hand.

When you are ready, transfer one blade to the right hand by bringing the left hand down to the right. Bring the left arm back towards the target. Imagine your left arm is a rifle aimed at the target.

The right hand holds one shuriken at the right hip. It may seem difficult to acquire the correct throwing grip on the shuriken in this position, but with practice it will become natural.

To raise your right hand for throwing, slide it up the right side of your body until the inside of your throwing wrist is firmly pressed against the side of your head above your ear. This is called the anchor point. It is important to keep your hand at the anchor point when you begin the throw to ensure consistency in your wrist angle and attitude.

Put one blade in the right hand.   This is the ready position for throwing.

Slide it up at a down-angle so as not to stick yourself with the point. You want to hide the fact that you are going to throw it. You may want to watch your own shadow and see if you can minimize the visible movement. Keep your right elbow in close. Keep your wrist cocked back so that the shuriken remains pointing up like an antennae. When the shuriken is raised, face the palm inwards and adopt a posture that conceals the shuriken within the hand. The shuriken should not be exposed until it is actually thrown.

As much as possible, you don't want to reveal to the opponent that you have a shuriken and are preparing to throw it at him. If he sees it, he will evade it.

When you are ready to throw, you will take a half-step forward with the left foot. At the same time you pull your left hand back to your left hip and swing your throwing hand across your body to meet your left hand at your left hip. The throwing arm moves in a circular motion and is only stopped when it strikes the left hip. You may want to practice without any shuriken, trying to slap your left hip with your right hand.

Do it so that the slap makes a noise and the movement is smooth.

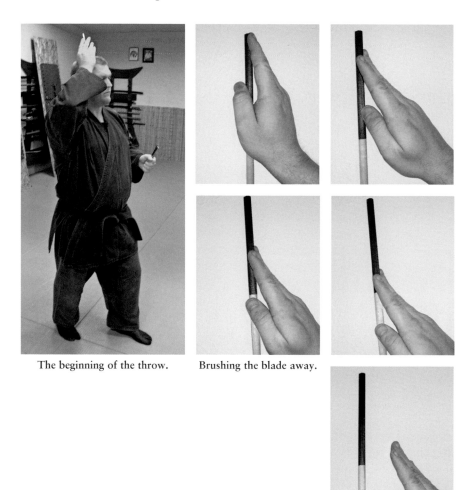

The beginning of the throw.   Brushing the blade away.

During the throw, keep your throwing hand cocked back so that the shuriken points at the sky throughout the throw. The shuriken will slide out of your hand, you do not "let go." As it slides away, you will brush the back of the blade with your fingertips to control its rotation.

Do not try to "throw" the shuriken and do not extend your arm towards the target. The wrist stays vertical and the arm moves in a circle. This seems to be difficult for many people, so have someone observe you during practice to make sure that you are doing it correctly. Even an untrained eye can tell you if your shuriken is pointed straight up, if your wrist stays cocked back, and if your right arm is moving smoothly to your left hip during the throw.

| Follow through on the throw. | Getting the next blade ready to throw. |

If your right hand does not strike your left hip at the end of the throw, then you threw incorrectly. If you are a beginner, it is not important whether or not the shuriken sticks in the target. What matters is acquiring a feeling for the movement of the throw. The desire to sink your blades into the target is very strong and perfectly understandable, after all, that's why we do it, but that desire is something you will have to control if you want to be successful. It seems like a contradiction, but budo is full of contradictions that you must simply accept and learn from. Follow the form and eventually you will have a "eureka" moment and the blades will start sticking.

After the first shuriken has been thrown, you should find both of your hands together at your left hip. At this time, you take the next shuriken from your left hand into your right hand.

Then, you step back into your original throwing position with the left arm straight towards the target and the right hand pressed into the side of your head. You will repeat this process until you have thrown your last shuriken.

When you are training, you may throw all of your shuriken. In a fight, you should never throw the last shuriken. You keep it so that you will have a weapon for *shoken-jutsu*. In a way, all but one of your shuriken are for throwing. One of them must be thought of as unthrowable. Of course, you never know what's going to happen, maybe you'll have to throw it, but it is always a good idea to hold something back.

After the last shuriken has been thrown in combat, you will draw your sword. This is the reason the right hand is brought to the left hip after each throw. The sword is carried at the left hip. After you throw the last shuriken in training, you will perform **zanshin**. Both hands are opened and the right palm faces up near the belly. Lean forward slightly and turn the right hand over. (Both palms down). Take a moment to "feel" the surroundings without looking or moving. Then, slowly, bring your arms up in front of you and make an "X."

Getting the next blade ready to throw.

This is similar to a *kamae* (posture) called *jumonji*. *Jumonji* means "In the shape of the number ten," which, in Japanese, is like an X (十). It is a Japanese tradition in martial arts to carry nine shuriken, so the number ten can mean "the end." (It doesn't matter how many shuriken you actually have).

Your position after the last blade is thrown.

Lean forward and turn the right hand over.

Form the *jumonji*.

Bow to the target.

After throwing it's important to maintain the feeling.

You assume the shape of *jumonji* to express the idea that the violence is finished. (*Jumonji* also happens to be a defensive posture one can use in hand-to-hand combat.) You might want to consider that, in a real fight, you may have just killed someone. Just because you are done fighting does not mean that the event is over for you. You will have to live with what you have done for the rest of your life. If you have really bad luck, you may have to live with it in prison.

After *jumonji*, stand up straight, feet together, fists on hips, and bow to the target.

Otsuke Sensei in *jumonji* after throwing his shuriken.

Before you walk to the target to retrieve your shuriken, it is imperative that you make sure everyone else is finished throwing, lest a stray shuriken hit you! If it is safe, then you may approach the target and pick them up. Pull out the stuck shuriken first and then pick up the shuriken that are on the ground. (You never know when one will fall out and hit you in the back of the head.) Pick them all up and carry them in your right hand, point-down.

Depending on the teacher's wishes, you may be allowed to keep practicing or you may have to let someone else use the target. If that is the case, then you say, *kotae*, which means it is someone else's turn.

This is the basic throw. There are advanced levels that you will learn that will lead you to the secret of Someya Sensei's unsurpassed technique, but if any part of your basic throw is not mastered, you will never get there. Here is the basic kata once again, performed by Otsuka Sensei.

Shizentai

Take a Half-step

Transfer the Blades

Take Blades Out

Remove the First Blade

Keep Left Arm Straight

Keep the Blade Up

Start the Throw

Make Sure to Keep
the Wrist Vertical

Finishing the Throw

Taking the Next Blade

Starting the Next Throw

The Final Throw

The Hands Move Back

Lean forward With
the Palms Down

Go to *Jumonji*

Return to Shizentai

The Iga Ryu *teppan* can be thrown in a manner similar to the bo shuriken except for the release. During the release, your right hand will twist slightly clockwise and your index finger and thumb will do the brushing. You still have to keep your wrist at the proper angle and brush the back of the blade, but it will be much easier to do with these heavy, wide and aerodynamic shuriken. The blade flies with the flat side facing the target. The Iga Ryu blade is basically a wing and aerodynamic forces will help straighten it during flight. The feeling of throwing the Iga Ryu blade is very different from a bo shuriken, but once you get it, they seem very easy to throw, like paper airplanes. You may wish to have a special target used only for these blades, because they can cause a great deal of damage.

Advanced Meifu Shinkage Ryu Shuriken-jutsu: The Jissen Kata

The *jissen* kata (combat throw) is practiced from *shizentai*. That is, no stance is taken and the blades are not exposed before the throw begins. You stand facing the target with your hands at your waist. Suddenly, and without warning, you will throw a single blade at the target and return to *shizentai*. Your *kamae* and technique will happen in the blink of an eye and then disappear just as quickly. This is the reality of throwing a shuriken in combat. Standing in *kamae* before you throw is only for training. To do so in a real fight would tell the opponent your intentions and ruin any chance of your throw being effective.

There are two distinct *jissen* kata movements unique to the Meifu Shinkage Ryu. No other school of shuriken-jutsu employs them. These movements give the Meifu Shinkage Ryu an uncommonly fast, hard-hitting throw. I chose to keep these two movements in a separate chapter because the study of such advanced movements, if undertaken before the student has mastered the basic throw, will slow down the progress of that student. The advanced movements rely totally on mastery of the basic throw. Keep this in mind.

The first movement is the wrist snap. The wrist snap is a method of "condensing" the throw into a smaller area. Instead of the entire body being involved in the throw, the movements are refined and forced into a smaller area of the body, the wrist. Of course, if any part of your technique is weak, then the condensed weakness will be very apparent.

To do the wrist snap, you begin the throw as normal. When you lift your foot to take that small step towards the target, your wrist will flex up so that the shuriken points down. When your foot hits the ground, your wrist will flex back the other way so that the shuriken is pointing up. Don't take a slower step; you must throw as fast as a normal footstep. The overall movement is very short and quick. Viewed from the side, the arm appears to undulate and crack like a bullwhip. In effect, you are creating a bullwhip, forcing an energy wave along a line segment. As the energy wave travels down your arm, the remaining length of your arm decreases, forcing the wave to accelerate. The arm will also tend to snap back towards you and sweep to the outside rather than to the inside. These are side effects of using a much faster and more powerful throw.

The wrist snap will create a much flatter trajectory for the shuriken and will increase penetration. It is also a strain on the arm and wrist; so don't push yourself to master it quickly. I would take a break every five throws.

Wrist Snap—Wrist Flexes Up

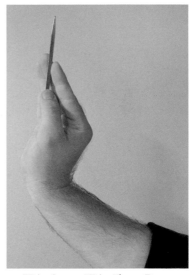

Wrist Snap—Wrist Flexes Down

The next movement in the *jissen* kata is the squeeze. Squeezing refers to the fingers and thumb of the throwing hand during the release. Your fingers and thumb will squeeze the blade into your palm. The fingers will slide down the back of the blade a few centimeters. This is basically a condensed form of the brushing you learned in the basic throw. It happens during the second half of the snap shot and is a very short, fast movement.

Beginning the Squeeze

Squeezing the Blade

The End of the Squeeze

Uchibari

The *uchibari* is very similar to the Meifu Shinkage Ryu type bo shuriken. It is lighter and has tapered ends, but the differences in size and shape are not sufficient to warrant a different method of throwing. The only actual difference is in the anchor point. You need to be careful in deciding what is and what is not an *uchibari*. The larger blades, blades over 2 ounces (60 grams), are most likely Katori Shinto Ryu shuriken and they are thrown from farther back on the head and without any snap. They have the same shape, but Katori Shinto Ryu blades are much thicker.

Katori Shinto Ryu blades run about 2¹/₂ ounces (70 grams), while *uchibari* run about 1¹/₃ ounces (38 grams) each.

Uchibari are singularly attractive blades, having a very sleek, sexy design. They were very popular, being claimed by several schools, including the Kukishinden Ryu and the Togakure Ryu.

Samples of the sleek looking *uchibari* blades.

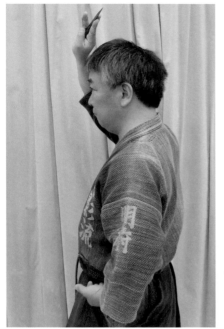

Preparing to throw the *uchibari*.   The *uchibari* anchor point is on the forehead.

The throw is the same basic bo shuriken method, but it starts from the front of the head and is a short, snappy movement.

How to grip the *uchibari*.

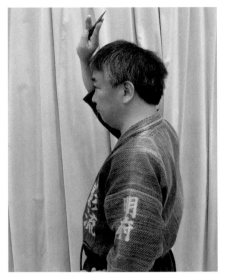

Start of the Throw

Beginning of the Release

Release

Follow-through

Chishin Ryu

Chishin Ryu blades are much heavier than Meifu Shinkage Ryu blades, with a wider base that tapers the entire length of the shuriken towards the tip. This design gives the blade a natural tendency to penetrate deeply. It can be a difficult blade to throw well, but of all the bo shuriken, this design is arguably the most lethal. This can be thrown *jikidaho* (direct throw) or *hantendaho* (reverse throw). The basic throw is not very different from a standard bo shuriken throw, but you may notice that there is no wrist snap and much less flexing of the arm. Also, note that the throw is done with the right foot forward and there is no step, just a shifting of balance forward. The heavier the blade is, the less you flex the wrist. Also, the heavier the blade is, the easier it is to brush it during the throw. These examples are 6 inches (16cm) long and weigh 3½ ounces (100g).

Chishin Ryu Blades

Chishin Ryu Grip

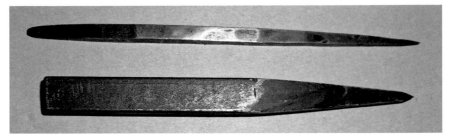

Here is a comparison between the *uchibari* (above)
and the much heavier Chishin Ryu (below).

Here is the basic throw in pictures. For heavier blades like this, the throw begins at the rear of the head, and maybe behind it.

Throwing the Chishin Ryu blade, step one.

Throwing the Chishin Ryu blade, step two.

Throwing the Chishin Ryu blade, step three.

Throwing the Chishin Ryu blade, step four.

Shirai Ryu

Shirai Ryu blades are exceptionally long blades of round stock, like big needles. Because they have no facets and are so long (around 8 inches or 21cm) the hand is used in a unique way during the throw. The fingers guide and control the upper part of the blade, as usual, but the inside of the wrist is also employed, cupping the bottom of the blade. The shuriken makes a sort of

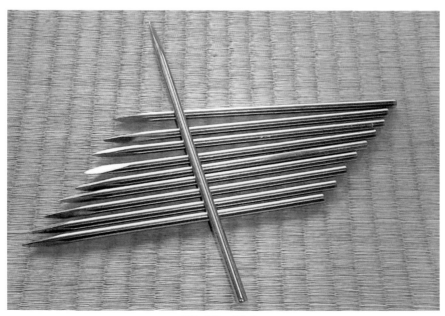

Shirai Ryu Blades

"bridge" between the fingertips and the notch in your wrist that forms when the thumb is closed. During the throw itself, you have to push on the bottom of the blade with your wrist and palm. These are long blades; they need a lot of brushing. You must keep your wrist vertical until after the blade is gone from your hand. Throwing these long, slender blades feels somewhat like running a length of rope across your hand. It has that kind of feeling.

Throwing the Shirai Ryu blade as seen from the front.

From the side you can see how far back the hand goes that's holding the blade.

As the arm moves forward the brushing begins.

The Shirai Ryu Blade has left the hand and is heading towards the target.

Follow through on the throw allows for the selecting of the next blade held in the hand.

Nage-ya Shuriken

Nage-ya literally means "throwing arrow" or "dart." There is a specific Japanese weapon referred to as a *nage-ya*, but I have chosen to use *nage-ya* to refer to a whole category of aerodynamic throwing weapons. In this instance, "dart" means a throwing weapon whose flight characteristics are intentionally modified by its design—notably tail fins, bristles, fletchings or a wrapping of cloth, string or paper. *Nage-ya* are also usually tapered towards both ends. (Compare Meifu Shinkage Ryu and Kono Ryu shuriken) These are both bo-shuriken, but they are sufficiently different in design to merit a separate category.

The *Nage-ya* or *Uchi-ne*

Kono Ryu shuriken

The bo shuriken, if it is not perfectly (or luckily) thrown, will not stick. The dart, *nage-ya*, does not depend entirely upon the skill of the thrower in order to fly straight and penetrate the target. The *nage-ya*, to varying degrees, will self-correct in flight, increasing the chances of success. You might think that such a design would be the best choice and see no reason for the more difficult bo shuriken, but *nage-ya* are larger, heavier and more expensive than bo shuriken, which means you'll be able to carry fewer of them. There is another reason: If you ever need to throw something that is not a shuriken, you will find objects that fly like bo shuriken very common, but dart-like objects will be somewhat rare. Having said that, *nage-ya* do tend to cause more damage than bo shuriken because of their heavier weight and broader points.

Negishi Ryu Blade

Not every dart has a particularly effective aerodynamic design. Some ideas worked better than others. As always, the design will depend on the source material, the intended purpose and the amount of craftsmanship involved. The modern toy dart is a perfect throwing tool. The weight is distributed forward, the tail is light and provides maximum surface area and the tip is slender, sharp and hardened. It takes very little skill to throw one and cause it to stick into an object. The only problem with it is that it was intended only to penetrate a few millimeters and cause only a minimal amount of damage. If it were heavier and had a larger tip, it would be a formidable throwing weapon. Indeed, there were some shuriken that evolved into designs that very closely resemble modern darts. (See *Juji-gata* shuriken)

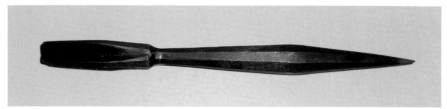

Juji-gata shuriken look very similar to modern darts.

Because of the increased weight and the effectiveness of the stabilizers (tail fins) these types of shuriken require a different throwing technique to maximize their chance at success. The throw does not appear to be very different from that of a standard bo shuriken, but it is different in several important ways.

The blade is gripped differently, sitting in the hand between the first and third fingers, as opposed to the first and second. The thumb rests against the tail, which provides better retention in the hand than a bo shuriken.

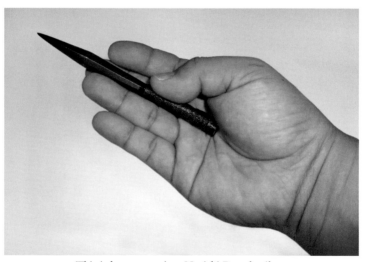

This is how you grip a Negishi Ryu shuriken.

The throw also differs in that the shuriken is held against the side of the head with the palm facing out. As the body moves forward, the elbow leads the throw, not the hand and the hand sweeps from the outside to the inside in a very circular movement. There is no snap shot possible with a dart. It would disrupt the flight of the blade and ruin the shot.

Negishi Ryu

All of the *nage-ya* type blades are thrown with a larger, slower throw than the smaller bo-shuriken. Heavier blades require a slower, more circular throw.

There are numerous pictures of Negishi Ryu blades in this book, so the shape ought to be familiar, but the throw is very different to what we have discussed. In many ways it is the opposite of the standard bo shuriken throw. To begin with, the body does not face the target squarely, as with the Meifu Shinkage Ryu. It is angled away from the target at 60 degrees. The palm faces out before the throw. Once the throw begins, the elbow leads the movement and when the hand moves, it sweeps from the outside in. There is some brushing required but not nearly as much as with a regular bo shuriken. As a matter of fact, the body moves so much differently with Negishi Ryu type blades, we often switch from one type to another during practice when our muscles become fatigued. One set of muscles for one kind of blade, one set of muscles for another. In the photos, pay attention to the initial hand position, the leading of the elbow and the final position of the hand, which is cocked back towards the rear more than with any other shuriken.

Throwing the Negishi Ryu blade, step one

Throwing the Negishi Ryu blade, step two

Throwing the Negishi Ryu blade, step three

Throwing the Negishi Ryu blade, step four

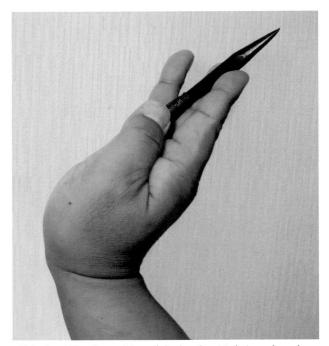

This should be the position of the hand as it's being released.

Be careful not to assume that, because the last picture shows Otsuka Sensei's hand pointing forward, that this is the end of the arm's movement —it is not. The arm keeps moving in a smooth arc to the left hip. If you were to stop the arm at this point it would ruin the throw and rob the shuriken of a great deal of energy.

Shaken

There were dozens of *shaken* designs, many of which had different purposes. Some were purely throwing weapons, some for hand-to-hand and throwing and some were used to deliver burning fuses, secret messages and even poison. Most had four points, some had 5, 6 and even 8 points, but the more points there were, the more difficult it was to throw and the less damage the shuriken would cause. There are two main kinds of *shaken* shuriken: Piercing blades and cutting blades. Piercing blades are made of thicker metal (.1 to .2 inches/4mm to 6mm) and have longer, more slender points. Cutting blades are made of thinner metal (.03 to .07 inches/1mm to 2mm) and often have smaller, knife-like points. Some are designed only to "stick," some are designed only to cut. All *shaken* are capable of piercing or cutting. When we refer to cutting or piercing, we refer to the nature of the wounds they create in human flesh, not to their performance in practice targets. This is not a sport; these are not sporting goods. Never judge the capability of a weapon solely by its performance on inanimate target materials.

The *shaken* is often thought of as an "easy" weapon to throw. It is in fact easier to stick in the target because of its many points, but developing power and accuracy in the throw is, in the author's opinion, more difficult than with the bo shuriken. Because of their wider, more dangerous shapes, *shaken* are also more difficult to carry than bo shuriken. The traditional number of blades to be carried was nine, but anyone who thought they would actually need a lot of shuriken would carry as many as they could.

The *shaken* with holes in the center could be strung together with a piece of cord. The *shaken* without holes could be carried between the folds of the wide obi (sash) worn around the waist. A samurai might only carry two or three but a ninja might carry more than a dozen, secreted in various pockets all over his body.

Senban shuriken can be carried by tying them to a cord or rope.

For a ninja, the shuriken was far more than just a throwing weapon. The manner in which it was carried could serve a purpose. If the shuriken were placed in pockets over vital areas such as the chest, the back of the neck or the forearms, then they would serve as a kind of secret armor against sword cuts. They could be tied to the soles of their shoes as a kicking weapon. In these cases, they did not have to serve with 100% effectiveness; they only needed to work well enough to help you survive. Remember that Japanese armor was made of iron plate about .03 inches (1mm) thick. A *shaken* was usually .03 to .07 inches (1 to 2mm) thick. It would stop a sword cut just as well as any armor of that time and place.

Senban shuriken can be used as secret armor when tied together along the arm.

The method of throwing both kinds of *shaken* is similar, but with a few differences owing to the different weights and shapes. The Meifu Shinkage Ryu is primarily a bo shuriken school, but Someya Sensei did train with a kind of *juji shaken*, (cruciform shuriken) a piercing blade that was popular with many of the old budo schools. That throw will be presented here. Then we will have a look at the *senban* throw of Togakure Ryu (a cutting blade).

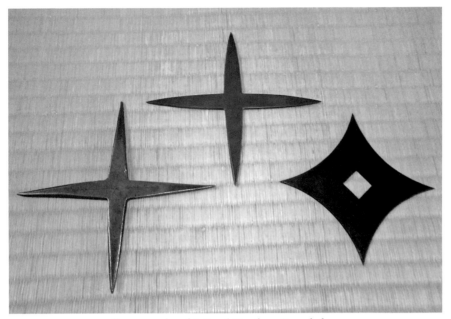

Some samples of *Juji* and Togakure Ryu *shaken*.

The basic grip resembles the "pistol" gesture: index finger straight, the rest of the fingers curled in. The tip of the index finger should lie just over the forward edge (not point) of the shuriken. This grip applies to almost any *shaken*. The index finger and the wrist cause the blade to spin, not the movement of the arm.

The *juji shaken* does not have cutting edges so the release for that blade is simpler than the Togakure Ryu *senban*. The Togakure Ryu *senban* requires a turning of the hand to keep the rear edges from slicing the palm as it flies away.

Juji Shaken

The *juji shaken* is thrown in a simple overhand manner. The grip is simple. The bottom three fingers wrap around the lower blade and the index finger covers just enough of the horizontal blade to make sure the *shaken* is aligned with the target during the throw. There is no need to spin the *juji shaken* rapidly due to its thickness (6mm). It has piercing type points as opposed to cutting points. It does need to spin a little, however, to fly accurately. The index finger creates spin by pulling down slightly on the forward-facing blade of the shuriken during the throw.

An impressive display of *juji shaken.*

How to grip the *juji shaken*.

The start of the throw.

The *juji shaken* as it is being released.

The position of the hand after
the *juji shaken* has been released.

Beginning of *juji shaken* throw.

The arm starts its movement forward.

The *juji shaken* just as
it is being released.

The hand and arm follow through
and prepare for the next throw.

Juji Shaken

Togakure Ryu Senban

The Togakure Ryu *senban* is a much thinner (.06 inches/1.6mm) piece of metal than the thick *juji shaken* (.23 inch/6mm). It is more of a cutting weapon than a piercing weapon. Because of this, and its light weight, it needs to be spun very rapidly in flight. The throw is much smaller and faster than a *juji shaken*. These blades, because of their light weight and thin profile, are also capable of being thrown side-hand very effectively.

They are often employed in greater numbers than the thicker, larger piercing-type *shaken*. As many as a dozen are drawn and held in the left hand in preparation for the right hand to draw them, one or two at a time, and throw them.

First we will look at the overhand throw and then we will discuss the sidehand throw.

Senban.

Beginning of the Throw   Mid-Throw   The Release

The upper arm and wrist snap forward and back, moving as little as possible. You don't want your arm to move too far forward or the blade will go into the ground. Try not to let your upper arm move at all during the throw. Snap the wrist forward and back about 10 inches (25 cm) at most. As you snap the wrist forward, your hand is going to turn inward so that your palm is facing you and your thumb is pointing up. The hand is turned inwards to allow the *senban* to clear your thumb without cutting you. As long as you don't try to "hold" the *senban*, but merely allow it to "perch," the blade will not turn inwards with your hand. It will keep rotating and fly straight to the target. Try to think of your hand as a "tool" that simply propels and spins the blade, not as a hand that is gripping and releasing something. It might even help to visualize one of those skeet throwers—it does not "hold" the skeet, it merely casts it.

Throwing Grip   Mid-Throw   Release Hand Position

Below is the overhand *senban* throw again, this time with no blade. Notice how, as the wrist snaps forward, the palm turns to the inside. If the palm does not turn, the bottom point will cut you as the blade begins to spin. Before the throw, the thumb is on the left hand side of the blade. As the throw begins, the thumb moves to the center. At the end of the throw, the thumb is all the way to the right.

The most common problem you may encounter is moving your arm too much during the throw. Note the short distance the arm moves in the pictures below.

Senban Throwing Grip

Mid-Throw

Senban Release

To counter this, you may train with your left arm horizontal in front of your chest. Keep it in place as a "bumper" for your right arm. Eventually you will be able to throw without even touching your left arm.

Use the non-throwing arm as a bumper.

Releasing the *Senban*

The sidehand throw is somewhat unique to the Togakure Ryu. It is a very surreptitious movement where the throw is completed close to the body and hidden by the sleeves. In order for the shuriken to fly accurately sidehand, it must be spun very quickly. Hatsumi Sensei recommends practicing the throw with business cards. First we will look at the grip and then the throw from in front and behind the thrower. The reason we will look at the throw from behind is to see how the body and the arms hide the throw. Done properly, the throw will be invisible from behind and hard to see from in front.

To begin, the *senban* should be held in the left hand, pressed against to the body. The right hand should also be kept pressed into the belly, low and inconspicuous. The right hand will slide the top *senban* off into the right palm and form the *tenouchi*.

Hold *senban* in the left hand.

Slide out the first *senban*.

The sidehand grip is formed by supporting the underside of the *senban* with the side of the middle finger, pressing down with the thumb and "hooking" the side of one point with the index finger. Be careful where you put the index finger. The *senban* will rotate around the index finger. This is what gives the sidehand throw such a high rate of spin. It does not rotate on its point, however. It rotates around the side of the point where it pushes against the finger. If you put your finger on the point, it will cut you when you throw it.

The sidehand grip for the *senban*.

The sidehand throw in mid-throw.

The sidehand throw's release position.

The right wrist then snaps quickly in the direction of the target. It is important to remember that this throw is a hidden movement, so if your target is to your left, you need to turn your body to the left to hide the throw. The elbow should stay in contact with your body during the throw. What makes the Togakure Ryu sidehand throw so unique is that it is the only shuriken throwing method that requires the arms to stay low, close to the body and well below the armpits.

The right wrist then snaps quickly in the direction of the target. It is important to remember that this throw is a hidden movement, so if your target is to your left, you need to turn your body to the left to hide the throw. The elbow should stay in contact with your body during the throw. What makes the Togakure Ryu sidehand throw so unique is that it is the only shuriken throwing method that requires the arms to stay low, close to the body and well below the armpits.

How the sidehand throw looks from the front.

We don't want any movement visible from the rear, and only minimal movement from the front. Note in the pictures above how the wrist turns but the arm moves very little and stays close to the body. This is unusual for any kind of throwing weapon. What this does for the thrower is to make his shuriken a complete surprise to the opponent, magnifying the power of a piece of metal into a weapon of tremendous psychological impact.

You should follow the formal routine for throwing bo shuriken when you throw *shaken*. *Shaken* are dangerous weapons, more dangerous than bo shuriken, and need to be treated with the same respect you would afford a firearm. A throwing routine helps eliminate random and unpredictable movement. If you drop one, the probability of it sticking in someone's foot is 300% higher than if you dropped a bo shuriken. Their many points snag on skin and clothing all too easily. All shuriken need to be kept off of the floor and out of the way when not in use.

The sidehand throw seen from behind.

Teppan

Teppan shuriken are the category of blades that could be any size or shape of blade made out of sheet metal. Some of them are quite aerodynamic; some of them are decidedly not. They are usually much easier to fight with than they are to throw, but not always. They are also usually capable of more uses than a bo shuriken. They often have cutting edges as opposed to sharp points that can only pierce. In short, they serve a variety of useful, non-ballistic purposes exceeding any other kind of shuriken, but they may also be thrown. To throw them, the basic bo shuriken technique is fine. The weight and balance of each blade will be different, so your sensitivity needs to be developed to such a level that you can compensate during the throw. The Iga Ryu blade has a heavy tail, but it catches the wind well. At first it might seem impossible to throw but after some practice, it may seem to be the easiest. The Tsugawa Ryu blade, with its cutting edges, will go through most practice targets easily, but it can be difficult to control during the release.

Because of their design, *teppan* are also very good at being combined or lashed to other objects in order to create a new weapon or tool, such as an animal trap.

Samples of expedient weapons made from *teppan*.

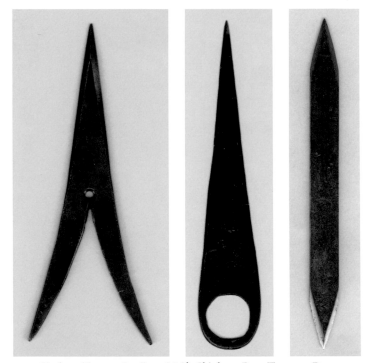

Various *Teppan*: Iga Ryu, Meifu Shinkage Ryu, Tsugawa Ryu

One rare kind of *teppan* worthy of note is the *senbakoki* blade. A *senbakoki* was a rice-threshing tool in use throughout Japan for hundreds of years. It is a wooden frame that supports a dozen or more 13-inch (35cm) long blades of triangular cross-section. The blades of the *senbakoki* have apparently been used to construct many kinds of weapons, including shuriken. *Senbakoki* shuriken can be thrown in the same manner as Tsugawa Ryu shuriken.

Senbakoki blades on the threshing tool.

Shuriken made from a *senbakoki* blade.

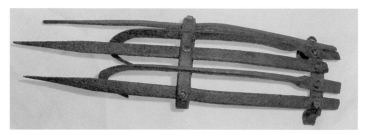

A *Tekagi* (fighting claw) made from *senbakoki* blades.

Kunai

There is one other type of Japanese weapon that could be called a *teppan*, but it is not normally considered a shuriken because of its size: the *kunai*. The *kunai* is basically a flat piece of metal with a handle and a leaf-shaped blade. They can be smaller than some large shuriken or as large as a short sword. The *kunai* is a kind of multi-tool, roughly made from iron plate (*teppan*) with unsharpened edges. The point was sharp and the edges would be rough from the *kunai* being used to shatter plaster and wood, to dig in rocky soil or as a prybar. It was not a knife; it was not made of tempered steel or polished. It was a cross between a garden trowel, axe and prybar. Ordinarily, this would not be considered a shuriken at all, but it certainly can be thrown and with devastating results. The method of throwing a *kunai* is the same as that for throwing a Japanese knife or sword. You grasp the handle like a knife and throw it like a knife, but during the release you also push with the palm. Pushing (or brushing) the handle with the palm and index finger slows the rotation of the blade, just as brushing with the fingers slows the rotation of a shuriken. It is the same principle, but on a larger, slower scale.

Samples of a large and medium sized *kunai.*

Tsugawa Ryu

The Tsugawa Ryu blade can be thrown in a fashion nearly identical to any bo-shuriken. The blade is gripped with it flat against the fingers, not the edge. (Don't forget this blade has an inch of sharpened cutting surface on both sides at each end.) As the blade leaves the hand, you brush the flat with the middle finger.

The beginning of throwing a Tsugawa Ryu blade (*kamae*).

Tsugawa Ryu blade, starting the throw.

The arm moves forward.

The Tsugawa Ryu blade being released.

The follow-through after the release.

Iga Ryu

The Iga Ryu can be thrown in a manner similar to the bo shuriken except for the release. During the release, your right hand will twist slightly clockwise and your index finger and thumb will do the brushing. You still have to keep your wrist at the proper angle and brush the back of the blade, but it will be much easier to do with these heavy, wide and aerodynamic shuriken. The blade flies with the flat side facing the target. The Iga Ryu blade is basically a wing and aerodynamic forces will help straighten it during flight. The feeling of throwing the Iga Ryu blade is very different from a bo shuriken, but once you get it, they seem very easy to throw, like paper airplanes. You may wish to have a special target used only for these blades, because they can cause a great deal of damage.

This is how you grip the Iga Ryu blade.

Starting position for throwing Iga Ryu blade.

The Iga Ryu blade in mid-throw.

The follow-through after releasing
the Iga Ryu blade.

Combat Techniques

The art of throwing shuriken has always been closely associated with the use of the sword. To teach the integration of the two arts, there are many kata for us to study. All of these exercises can be done with one or two shuriken. You can throw the second shuriken either before or after the first cut. These exercises come from the Meifu Shinkage Ryu. Before you begin, take a moment to calm yourself and become still inside. Try not to think about what you are going to do before it happens. Let throwing and cutting happen on their own, not as expressions of desire to perform well, (this is not a performance art or a sport) or as the execution of plans you have made for the immediate future. Throwing and cutting must be spontaneous, without premeditation, from the void.

(Despite Otsuka Sensei's estimation of my skills, I am NOT particularly skilled in the use of the *katana*. I apologize for my imperfect form. The important thing to note is how the shuriken is incorporated into the ordinary use of the sword.)

1. *Ipponme Zaho* (Throwing and Cutting From a Seated Position)

With your sword sheathed, sitting in *seiza*, covertly slide your throwing hand up to your head with a minimum of observable movement. Throw the shuriken at the target. At the end of the throw, your throwing hand will grasp the handle of your sword. Rise up and take a step with your right foot as you draw and cut horizontally to the throat of the opponent. Slide your left leg underneath you. Take another step with your right foot as you cut again straight down to the head. Sheathe your blade and return to *seiza*. Cutting and stepping should take place at the same time.

Sit Calmly

Throw

Draw Sword

Cut and Step

Move Up

Cut Down

2. *Ipponme* (Throwing and Cutting From a Standing Position)

As with #1, your right hand will throw a shuriken. Draw the sword at the end of the throw and cut upwards across the chest (*kesa*). Step forward with the left foot and thrust to the throat, resting the back of the blade in the crook of your left elbow. (Be careful!) Step back with the left foot as you cut back down across the chest.

Shizen

Prepare

Throw and Draw

Cut Upwards

Prepare for Thrust

Thrust

Cut Downwards

Finish

3. *Nihonme* (Throwing From the Draw)

From a standing position, step back with the left foot and prepare to draw and cut with your sword. When you grasp the sword, take a shuriken from the left hand and throw it instead. After you throw the shuriken, draw the sword and cut. There are two variations to this technique. You may do it as written, or you may grasp the sword with the right hand and throw the shuriken with your left hand before drawing the sword. In either case, both hands need to be on the sword when you draw for practical and safety reasons.

Start the Draw

Throw the Shuriken

Complete the Draw

Cut

Sanbanme (Throwing During a Cut)

From a standing position, draw the sword with a shuriken in your right palm. Hold the sword in *jodan* or *hasso no kamae*. With the intention of cutting, release the sword with the right hand and hold it with your left hand as you throw the shuriken hidden in your right palm. Alternately, as in the photos, you may draw a shuriken from some other location, such as the collar.

The Tsugawa Ryu blade can be hidden in the collar.

Start with *hasso no kamae*.

Reach behind and draw the blade.

Move the sword aside as you throw.

Follow through with the throw.

Henka-uchi (Unconventional Throwing Methods)

These are the methods of throwing the shuriken in an unforeseeable manner; a surprise throw that does not exhibit obvious throwing movements that could be recognized. These techniques come from the various physical situations of everyday life, such as eating, walking and even sleeping.

Gyaku-uchi

The Cross Throw. The hand starts near the opposite side of the body, as though the arms were crossed, and travels horizontally during the throw. This is a fast, hard-to-see movement.

This is the stance for *Gyaku-uchi*.   How the blade is thrown using *Gyaku-uchi*.

Shitate-uchi

The Underhand Throw. While walking or standing naturally, the shuriken is thrown from behind the hip. The hand will snap back after the release. Be careful not to accidentally throw the shuriken to the rear.

Blade position in *shizentai*.	Throwing the blade underhand.	Snap the hand back.

Za-uchi

The Seated Throw. While in *seiza*, the shuriken are held in the left hand at the left hip. The right hand, holding one blade, sits at the right hip. One must be very still and refrain from moving until the moment of the throw. When you are ready, then the right hand slides up the body, point down, and towards the target in one smooth motion. Be careful not to rise up off the legs or lean too far forward. As soon as the throw is finished, return to your original position and be absolutely still.

Unlike the standing throw, the left arm does not point towards the target. You will use the left hand to push down against your left hip or thigh to provide power to the throw that the left leg normally provides when standing. This is true for any sitting throw.

Sit quietly in *seiza*.

Slide the blade up the chest.

Bring blade to starting position.

Then throw the blade.

Iza-uchi

Throwing From a Chair. This technique as almost identical to *za-uchi*. The trick is to rest lightly in the chair, allowing both heels to float. Your hands start out in your lap, under the table. When you throw, use the balls of your feet to control your body. Be careful not to strike the underside of the table when you raise the shuriken to throw. As with *za-uchi*, you slide the blade up your body.

Seated at a table.

Slide the blade up to the head.

Aim at your target and throw the blade.

Release the blade towards target.

Aruki-uchi

Throwing while walking. Facing the target and from mid-stride, throwing the blade is relatively straightforward. Walking past a target or at an angle to the target is more difficult. One must turn the body from the hips as one throws. This takes much practice but is a valuable skill to have.

Ne-uchi

Ne-uchi means throwing from a sleeping position. Try to relax as though you really are sleeping and close your eyes. Open your eyes, lift your head to see the target and then throw the shuriken. Before you throw the next shuriken, put your head back down on the floor and close your eyes. You want to practice from a "sleeping" state, not just lying down. (Be aware that your legs and crotch are now in a vulnerable position should your shuriken bounce off the target.)

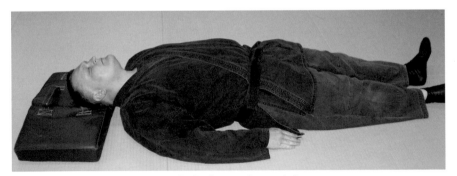

To practice *ne-uchi*, lie down, relax, and close your eyes.

Wake up and bring the blade to the start position.

Complete the throw at your target.

There are other techniques that will aid your ability to survive, but we don't necessarily need to worry about proper Japanese names nor formal methods for practice. Here are a handful of the most common:

Two Shuriken in One Hand—As the title suggests, you hold two shuriken in one hand and throw them in succession or at the same time. The grip is different depending on which method you choose. If you throw two at once, there will be more of a shocking effect on the opponent, but penetration will decrease as the arm is having to throw twice the weight at the same time, slowing the blades down. If you throw them in succession, you can get the same depth of penetration, but learning to do this well takes effort.

Grip for throwing two blades in succession.

Decoy Throw—Once you master the art of throwing two shuriken from the same hand in succession, then you can throw a decoy shot. The first shuriken is thrown slowly, in an upward fashion, towards the face. It will easily be seen and avoided by the opponent, but the second shot will come down fast and hard while he is busy avoiding the first blade. The first blade does not need to be thrown well; it is merely a distraction, but if you can stick the first shot, do it.

Feints—This is a simple technique wherein you pretend to throw your shuriken, disturbing the opponent and weakening his ability to perceive the real attack.

Throwing With Both Hands—You may throw shuriken from either hand, either in succession or at the same time. It is always a good idea to train both hands as you never know when one hand will become injured, but being able to rain shuriken down on the opponent is also a good thing. Keeping some shuriken on both sides of your obi, you can continuously draw and throw shuriken from both hands without stopping until you are out of blades. When your hand finishes the release of one blade, instead of pointing at the target, it draws another from your belt. You are not limited to merely having blades on both sides of the belt. You can draw them from behind your neck, inside your jacket, and any other place. Just remember that the end of each throw is the draw for the next for that hand.

Wearing shuriken on both sides.

Ready to begin.

First blade is thrown and
the second is at the ready.

The second blade is thrown
and the third is at the ready.

The third is thrown and
the fourth is at the ready.

Piercing the Ground—If you were fighting on wooden flooring, as Japanese castles and shrines have, you could throw and stick a shuriken in the planks near the feet of your opponent. Obviously, sticking the blade in his feet would be more effective, but if you should miss, you might want to consider the effect that it will have on his mind. Do not consider it a defeat. He will not know if you meant to strike his foot or the ground, so keep your poker face (75% of budo is psychology)! The sound of a shuriken sticking into wood can be quite loud and disconcerting, especially when it is close to your feet. The protruding blade has now become an obstacle to his smooth footwork, which could cause a swordsman to lose his balance. Also, you might wish to intimidate someone of unknown intentions without causing injury.

Rolling and Throwing—You should practice *ukemi* (rolling) and throwing. You can throw before you roll, as you begin to roll, during the roll and after the roll. Shuriken dojos often have slick flooring, so be careful not to slide into the target when you roll. Do not get disoriented and throw the blade in the wrong direction.

Yadone (Yah-doe-nay), **arrow and shuriken avoidance**—This is a very rare skill, taught and practiced by only one or two schools in Japan. Basically, you use a sword, spear, staff or even a bow to shield yourself as you avoid incoming arrows or shuriken. The idea is simple, but it is difficult to master. When you know there is a blade coming in, turn your body to the side and hold your sword out in front of you with the blade sideways in your hand. You then divide the world into two halves in your mind. There is one half to the right of the sword and one half to the left. When the opponent launches a weapon at you, you must decide which half it will occupy. When you think you know which one, move to the other half. You move your body, but you ***do not move the sword at all***. It must stay perfectly still. You do not attempt to block or strike the incoming blades with your sword. If they do strike it, that is fine, but of no consequence.

Your sword can help you identify the direction of your movement when dodging shuriken.

If you move too soon, he will see it and strike you. If you try and block with the sword, he will use decoys and feints. If you hold the sword too high, he will throw at your legs and feet.

Shoken-jutsu (Hand-held Techniques)

Shuriken-jutsu (掌剣術) is not merely throwing blades or striking a target. The hand-to-hand techniques of the shuriken are really no different from any small weapon techniques. The philosophy behind it is a little different, however. The blade is to be kept hidden from the attacker at all times. Since the shuriken is a small weapon and without cutting edges, it is best used to amplify the effects of empty-handed techniques. A shuriken could be used to stab someone in the throat, and that is indeed one of the written techniques. A shuriken could also be used to turn a pinch into something unimaginably painful. A shuriken can turn a punch into a deep puncture. Shuriken can even be used to trap weapons or fingers and twist the opponent painfully onto the ground.

The shuriken can be used for hand-to-hand fighting.

The first thing you should consider is the small size of a shuriken. They are not weapons meant to be used openly against other weapons. You should move as though you have no weapon at all. Only then will you receive the benefits of a small weapon like a shuriken. If someone strikes at you, don't think of blocking the attack. Evade the attack and move to a safe place. From that place of safety you may apply your shuriken to the opponent in a subtle way. You need not kill the opponent, but merely gain control of him. When studying these techniques, you ought to consider that a shuriken is not required—you could have a pencil or a pen or even a stick in your hand.

You may thrust at an enemy's vulnerable areas with the point of the blade. Alternatively, you can cut by dragging the point across the skin. Used deftly and secretively, the opponent will not know what is happening until it is too late. This is the art of *kakushi buki*, hidden weapons. The art of using hidden weapons is keeping weapons out of sight until the very end. If it is possible, keep them hidden even then and afterwards. The courage to wait until the last moment to use a weapon is a requirement of high-level shuriken-jutsu and is far more sophisticated than simply throwing a blade

Shoken-jutsu, small-weapon fighting, is for an enemy who is close to you. *Daken-jutsu*, throwing-blade fighting, is for an enemy who is out of reach.

That is not to say that you cannot throw a shuriken at an opponent who is very close to you. You certainly can and with great effect. With *daken-jutsu*, the shuriken master can utilize the empty space between himself and the opponent. With *shoken-jutsu*, the distance is zero and yet, you may still control it if you keep your weapons secret.

There are some specific hand-to-hand techniques, but really, the *waza* (techniques) themselves are not important. What matters are the concepts that run through them. We want the opponent to believe we are unarmed and non-aggressive. We want to avoid using any weapons until such time as they may be secretly employed. There are many considerations to be taken into account when using a weapon in self-defense, not the least of which may be the impressions of those who witness the fight. How you behave at such times may have ramifications beyond actual combat. If you are lucky enough to survive, you may have some legal troubles, depending on where you live and the laws of that country. Every country allows for its citizens to defend their own lives, but it will always be better to be seen as a victim who survived than a triumphant combatant.

Let's start by looking at various ways of holding a shuriken for hand-to-hand use. The shuriken may be held in a number of ways and you may also hold more than one, turning the fist into a spiked weapon capable of attacking in many directions.

The preferred method will always be the one that hides the blade from the opponent. In the photos, the blade is very obvious, but when you train, you should try to develop grips that hide the blade as much as possible. If you can keep the blade covered with cloth, such as your sleeve or a handkerchief, you will have the ideal *tenouchi* or *mochi*, which means "grip." Don't worry about the cloth, the point will go right through it like paper.

Junte Mochi is a stabbing grip. The index finger covers the blade and keeps it hidden while providing stability during a thrust.

Gyakute Mochi is also a stabbing grip; the classic icepick grip.

Juji Mochi, or "cruciform grip," gives you the ability to stab or punch with the blades. This grip is not well concealed but does provide lots of options.

Junte Mochi **No Ni** (*junte mochi* #2) is a means of utilizing the point of the blade to control the opponent by turning a simple pinch into an agonizing experience.

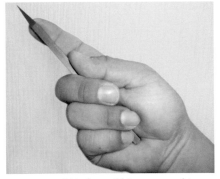
Junte mochi is for stabbing or punching.

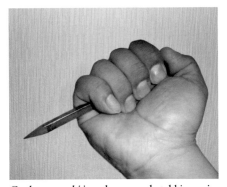
Gyakute mochi is a downward stabbing grip.

Juji Mochi grip is good for
punching and stabbing.

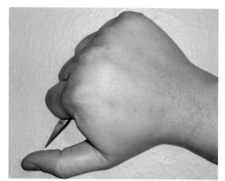

Junte mochi no ni is for pinching.

Here are some examples of shuriken being used in combat. They feature a simple bo shuriken, a Tsugawa Ryu blade and an Iga Ryu blade. At all times the movement is light and without force. Shuriken have sharp points; that is all the motivation the opponent will need to move the way you want him to move. Having said that, don't injure your training partner. People who often cause injuries to their training partners have a low level of skill. Budo IS control; controlling yourself.

Standing in *shizen* the bo shuriken is hidden.

Evade the cut, use shuriken to
control his hands.

Lift his right elbow and keep moving lightly.

Slide the shuriken up to his throat.

A small blade can do a great deal of damage.

Standing in *shizen*, the Tsugawa Ryu blade is hidden.

Step inside the cut and bring the shuriken up to the inside of his elbow.

Using the upper point, lift his elbow.

The blade's position when used to
raise the elbow.

Bounce the point down into his throat.

From *shizen*, the Iga Ryu blade
is hidden.

Evade the cut first, then
bring shuriken to his sword.

The Iga Ryu blade holding the sword.

Step forward and raise his sword.

Keep moving and raise the blade.

Bring the blade up to his neck.

You could also employ shuriken to increase your own defensive capabilities when using other weapons like the sword. You could tie the blades onto other weapons with a piece of rope or simply hold them in your hands in between the weapon and your palm. Some blades were actually designed for this purpose, such as the *shaken* of the Shinkage Ryu.

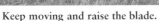

Shinkage Ryu *senban* have a hole for threading a cord.

Tsugawa Ryu blade and sword— *gyakute mochi*.

Holding a Meifu Shinkage Ryu blade in
juji mochi.

Tsugawa Ryu blade and
sword in *gyakute mochi.*

Here is the *junte mochi no ni* (pinch grip) in action. You get a piece of him and apply the point gently. It is important not to pinch too hard, or you may drive the sharp point through his skin and into your own thumb. If the point does penetrate his skin, move your thumb off to the side to protect yourself.

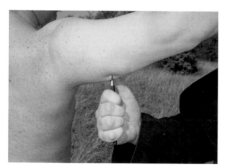

Use the thumb to push
some skin onto the point.

Hold your thumb steady and
let him do the damage to himself.

You may also use shuriken to increase the effectiveness of other martial arts techniques such as punches, throws and joint manipulations, such as *omote gyaku.* Be very careful with this aspect of training. Metal is totally unforgiving of human flesh and it will cut skin and break bones with only a little force.

Omote gyaku with an Iga Ryu blade.

Using the shuriken when attacked with a sword.

Insights

The Step

During the beginning movement of the throw, your upper body pulls slightly towards the rear and your weight transfers to your front leg. However, you must stay balanced and light on your feet. During the throw, a half step is sufficient. At the end of the throw, your upper body should not hang over your leading leg. Be careful not to lean over or twist your body to the point that your head goes past your front foot (a common error). Power will be robbed from the throw if the step forward is too large.

The heel of your stepping foot is allowed to make contact with the ground first. (Lightly…don't slam your feet into the ground.) That foot rolls onto the floor, heel to toe. If your foot just slaps onto the ground, it will disrupt the natural movement of the throw. (And you may fall over). The foot should roll onto the floor, allowing you to generate more power for the throw. You must allow your body to throw the shuriken and resist the urge to make it an action of merely the hand and eye.

Anchor Points

When you bring the shuriken up to your head to throw it, there are anchor points you can use, according to the type of shuriken you are throwing. By "anchor point" I mean the places on the head your wrist makes contact. If you are using a heavy shuriken, your anchor point should be at the rear of your head, behind and above the ear. Medium-sized shuriken, like Meifu Shinkage Ryu blades, should be held at the side, above the ear. Smaller shuriken should be held at the front of the head above the eyebrow. Also, when you are very close to the target, the more forward your anchor point should be, regardless of size. When you throw from the rear anchor point, your throw will be longer and slower. When you throw from the front anchor point, your throw will be shorter and faster.

The Throw

The throw is not merely a movement of the arm. It is a release of a spring created with the whole body. The arm moves from the right side of the head down towards the left hip. It moves in a natural arc and it is easy to concentrate the power of the whole body into the shuriken. Don't think about this too much; just keep it in mind when you practice.

Hand Development

The throwing hand will develop through practice. The muscles that squeeze the little finger and the thumb together will get bigger and stronger. These muscles increase the power and control of the grip, and this is necessary to develop the high-speed throw of the Meifu Shinkage Ryu. If you look at these pictures, you will see that Otsuka Sensei's hand muscles are so developed that he can pinch a shuriken or a pencil and hold it in the palm of his hand. This takes years of training.

Otsuka Sensei holding
a pencil.

Otsuka Sensei holding a shuriken.

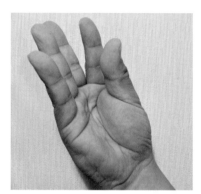

Hand Muscles of Otsuka Sensei

The Throwing Arm

Your throwing arm is attached to your body at the shoulder. Its movement is therefore circular. The shape of the throwing arm, however, is that of several angles. The elbow and the wrist are held at constant angles throughout the throw.

You do this to keep the shuriken vertical, pointed at the sky, all the way to the end and even after the shuriken has left your hand. If you let your arm go loose or your wrist bend forward, the shuriken will be affected by the circular movement of your arm and will spin uncontrollably away. This is a difficult thing to do for many people, but if you train slowly and let someone watch you from the side, then you can integrate it into your training. It might be useful to remember that we are not really "throwing" the shuriken, but rather casting the shuriken. Imagine that your arm is like a gear in a machine. It rotates from the shoulder, but it does not change its shape. Later on, you will learn the wrist snap and that does change the shape of the arm to a degree, but if you don't have this angular-arm concept down first, you will not be able to do the wrist snap properly. You MUST keep your wrist vertical throughout the entire throw.

This sequence demonstrates how to keep the wrist vertical during a throw.

The Left Hand

In the old days, the left hand of a warrior would rest constantly on the left hip, holding the sheath of his sword. The sword could be drawn at any moment, so the left hand was kept ready at all times. Please keep that in mind when you practice. Before you throw, the left arm is to remain straight. During the throw the left hand comes to the left hip, when you may take another shuriken with your right hand or draw your sword. The pulling back of the left hand to the left hip assists the body in throwing the shuriken. The left hand also assists the right hand during the snap shot. At the moment of the snapping of the right wrist, the left hand is also snapped back quickly to the body.

Both arms move at the same time, creating a smooth, natural throw. Remember to hold the extra shuriken lightly near the points. Gripping the centre of the blades makes them difficult to draw. When the shuriken are held in this manner, the tails of the blades spread out, creating the shape of an opened fan.

Extra shuriken held point-in, tails spread out.

Zanshin of the Meifu Shinkage Ryu

In many martial arts, there is a concept known as *zanshin*. *Zanshin* can be translated as "remaining spirit." Basically, this refers to the mental state of the student in the moments immediately following the completion of some technique. In sports, it may be acceptable to stop and observe the results of your actions to see how well you may have done. It may also be acceptable to express your emotions about your success or failure. In budo this is not an acceptable practice. You must remember that there will always be another enemy who comes along. It is never "over." Even when you have thrown all of your shuriken, you must remain in a state of preparedness. It makes no difference whether you stick all your blades in the center of the target or whether they all hit the floor. Training and fighting are the same. You must stay focused, alert and calm. You must maintain your *kamae* (posture) and your attitude. You neither congratulate nor berate yourself. Training is a kind of flow that continues regardless of the physical results of any given technique.

Zanshin has another meaning. It is a way of cultivating the determination necessary to survive in combat. This determination is very important to you as a student of budo. Without it, your training will be in vain. A strong spirit is more important than a trained body. This is what we mean when we say someone is a "natural warrior." Even without training, some people have this kind of spirit. Regardless of where you begin, however, that spirit must be cultivated through training.

Ideas for Practice

Correcting for height is relatively easy. To strike higher, release sooner. To strike lower, release later. If your shuriken are veering left or right, most likely it is because your grip is not correct or your wrist is bending during the throw. Have someone observe your wrist as you throw.

Strength and Weakness

Throwing the shuriken as hard as you can will not yield good results. Not only is it incorrect technique, it is dangerous: shuriken thrown with too much force will bounce off of the target and may strike you or an innocent bystander. Try instead to use only 50 percent of your strength.

This is not just "advice." People who consistently throw shuriken too hard and cause dangerous ricochets can be kicked out of the school if they fail to observe safe training procedures. I have seen it happen. Everybody makes mistakes from time to time, but consistently putting other students in danger by ignoring the teacher is unacceptable. Don't be one of those people and don't train anywhere near them. You only get two eyes and you don't want to lose one.

There are other kinds of strength besides sheer muscle. Once you gain the feeling for the throw, you will see how physical power should be applied. If you like a challenge, try throwing the shuriken with the absolute minimum amount of strength you can use. When throwing in slow motion, if your technique is not close to perfect, the shuriken will not stick in the target. Being able to stick a blade in the target without using any strength is fairly difficult, but if you can do it, then your powerful throws will be devastating. This is how you develop a powerful throw—training without power. Visitors to the dojo often stared at this training and assumed that we were beginners. Once Otsuka Sensei explained the difficulty and advanced nature of this kind of training, it became a challenge and many tried to do it, only to discover that very few of them could. Training slowly and with no muscle will teach you to throw naturally and correctly. This has nothing to do with how long you have been training. Beginners and advanced students should be training in this way.

Knowing the Distance

Knowing the distance between yourself and the target and how to throw the shuriken from that distance is a fundamental skill you must learn. You will learn it in practice over time. Many students want to measure their progress in distance from the target and that is fine, but your ultimate goal is to not consciously know the distance and still be able to hit the target every time. The body will learn this, not your mind. To improve this ability, take a step to the rear after each successful throw. When you reach your limit, start over from there and move closer to the target after each successful throw. Having said that, please understand that distance does not equal mastery. Yes, being able to throw from longer and longer distances is a sign that you are learning how to brush the shuriken well, but this is not mastery. Mastery is the ability to throw the shuriken hard, fast and straight with very little visible body movement. Your training should not be focused on distance from the target. Your training should be focused on the skills that will lead you to mastery. Train slowly, as slowly as possible.

Don't neglect practicing at close distances. The desire to advance in skill by throwing from longer distances should be ignored. That is not skill. Skill is knowing the distance wherever you may be and sometimes that means close enough to kiss. Remember to *wear eye protection* when you practice at close range .

Put Your Mind in the Blade

During practice, most beginners think about the target. They think about where they want the blade to go and they think about the blade sticking in that spot. This is incorrect. Eventually, your blades will naturally go where you want them to go and stick. During training, however, you need to put your awareness into the shuriken itself. Focus on the orientation of the blade throughout the throw and even as it flies through the air. It takes a considerable degree of concentration to teach the body how to throw a shuriken with precisely controlled rotation. Do yourself a favor and forget about the target completely, if you can. The sooner you do, the sooner you will find your blades piercing it with regularity.

Training, Targets and Safety

Safety is the most important thing, always. Safety for you and your fellow students and any observers must come before any other concerns. These are real, dangerous weapons that are designed to cause injury and death. Unlike many schools, we train with live weapons. Never lose your respect for any kind of weapon. They are not toys.

Keep your shuriken clean and devoid of rust or blackening chemicals. A small cut is one thing. A cut that introduces rust into the bloodstream can kill you. Blackening chemicals will give the shuriken a stickiness that can cause you to lose control of the blade during the throw, which is very unsafe. Please remove all rust and blackening chemicals with some kind of mild abrasive and coat the blades with a small amount of oil. When you are ready to throw, wipe off the oil. When you are finished, wipe the blades off and re-oil them. Reshape the tips with a fine stone when they become dull. Dull shuriken are more likely to bounce out of the target, which makes them more dangerous to you. When honing the tips, take your time, use gentle pressure and try to remove only the minimum amount of steel. Don't use a grinder!

Over the years, various ways of storing shuriken have been used. Cloth rolls, wooden boxes, eyeglass holders, pencil cases and other similar items work well. For some *shaken*, the old ten-pack floppy disk holders work like a charm. If you use a metal container, it might be a good idea to line the inside walls with felt to keep the points from being dulled. None of these containers will keep them completely rust-free, however, so take them out and clean them once in a while.

As for a training space—You will need a fairly high ceiling if you train indoors, preferably ten feet if you want to throw more than 10 feet. You will need lots of padding to protect the walls and floors behind and underneath your target. Tarps, blankets, foam padding, insulation and cardboard will suffice. During normal classes, we use squares of carpet and cardboard under a tarp to protect the floor. We use solid foam boards of wall insulation to protect the walls. At the training camps, we tend to use only tatami mats for targets and to protect the floors.

Formal target arrangement at a dojo.

Tatami targets at shuriken training camp.

Setting up portable targets for practice.

Stretch your wrists and fingers backwards for several minutes before throwing. Stretch your back and hip muscles as well.

Targets can take many forms. In Japan we use old tatami mats. As they get old, they get soft and make an ideal target. They are messy, however. Sometimes we use rubber jigsaw mats that are doubled up, about 1 inch thick. The target needs to be as tall as a man and wider than a man (about 6 feet by 3 feet). Please do not use wooden targets for bo shuriken. Wood tends to deflect bad throws with efficiency, increasing the danger to you and bystanders. They are also noisy and require a perfectly horizontal throw to stick. You don't want the blade to stick horizontally. Ideally, the tail should be pointing down a little bit in order to add to the penetration of the point. The blade rotates in flight, so if the blade strikes horizontally, it will slap the target upwards expending its energy with the tail. If the tail is pointed down a bit, that rotational energy will help drive the point in deeper.

For *shaken*, wooden targets are fine. Soft pine makes an excellent target. For the vertical throw, arrange the target with the grain vertical. For the side-arm throw, arrange the target with the grain horizontal. *Plywood and other hard substances are not recommended.* These weapons were designed to cut and penetrate skin and muscle, not dense materials.

Remember that it is great if your blades penetrate the target deeply, but as long as they strike point-first, even if they bounce out, then the throw was successful. These are weapons designed to cause injury and remaining in the wound does not increase the amount of damage. In general, a good throw will stick in a good target. Don't change your throw from what you have been taught in order to improve your chances of sticking the blades in a difficult target material. This is budo. Your real target is human skin, muscle and bone. Keep that in mind.

There are three ideal bull's-eyes on each target: Face/throat, hands/groin and the insteps of the feet. These three targets may represent different areas if you are throwing from a seated position against a seated opponent. Traditionally, these targets are indicated by a small black circle about 1 inch in diameter, but feel free to draw a human silhouette if you like. We did this in Japan and it quickly became the favorite target in the dojo. You may also consider other targets if you like. The kneecaps would make excellent targets, although they may be hard to hit. Try not to prejudge the value of various targets. The face/throat is a sensitive and potentially lethal target, but a wounded hand will make it difficult to wield a weapon. Wounded feet have difficulty walking. At sea level, the blood pressure in your feet is three times as high as the blood pressure in your head. They bleed profusely when cut. The wound pictured below was caused by *someone else's* ricocheting blade. If my foot had been the actual target, there would have been a lot more blood. In your training bag, it is a good idea to keep a supply of alcohol wipes and adhesive bandages. You will sustain small injuries in class; that is unavoidable when dealing with live weapons.

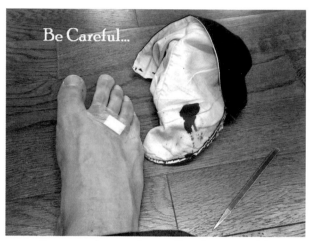

Feet can make a good target if you're not careful.

For beginners in the Meifu Shinkage Ryu, there are some special training methods available. The first method involves the use of specially constructed practice shuriken. They are simple to make. You need some small Styrofoam balls, chopsticks and rubber tubing. Cut the chopsticks down to 6 inches (15 cm) in length, insert them through a 5-inch (12 cm) piece of the tubing and push on the Styrofoam ball. With a partner, practice throwing them to each other. You are not trying to strike your partner, you are trying to throw the practice blade in such a way that the ball stays on top and the blade does not tumble or turn in the air. It's harder than it sounds, but it is excellent training.

Another good idea for beginners is "chopstick training." Otsuka Sensei devised this method of training his new students to feel the "brushing" of the fingers down the back of the blade. Chopsticks are much lighter than real shuriken, so developing the necessary sensitivity to throw a chopstick makes the real thing that much easier to do. All you need are some of the unlacquered wooden chopsticks of square cross-section and a foam bath mat. You may wish to slightly sharpen the points of the chopsticks and oil them to give them some weight. Once you have your target mounted, you may practice the basic throw. One of the great things about chopstick training is that it is almost impossible to cause serious property damage. You can still put out someone's eye, however, so treat them like weapons, because they are. Once you have mastered the basic throw with the training shuriken and the chopsticks, throwing the real shuriken should seem pretty easy.

These training shuriken can help students work on throwing techniques safely.

The Meifu Shinkage Ryu Research Group

Otsuka Sensei likes to refer to the Meifu Shinkage Ryu as a research group because we like to study the methods of schools other than our own. The Meifu Shinkage Ryu is a very informal school that welcomes students of other schools and often invites teachers from other schools to demonstrate their shuriken-jutsu. Members are allowed to practice the techniques of other schools and share them with the group. (Which is generally not accepted practice in traditional budo schools). Such things are acceptable only so long as the student remembers to show respect and loyalty to the school in which he finds himself. I struggled with this concept, afraid of offending my primary budo school by joining another school to learn shuriken-jutsu. Eventually, after discussing it with one of the *shihan*, I received a "dispensation," you might say, to train in another school.

The main activities of the Meifu Shinkage Ryu include weekly practice at a training hall in Tokyo, spring and autumn training camps and public demonstrations (*embu*). There are no Meifu Shinkage Ryu dojos outside of Japan as yet, but there are a few *keikokai* (training groups) in other countries now in other countries now (America, Belgium, Finland, Germany, and Spain). There may be some foreign dojo established soon, but nothing will ever take the place of training with the grandmaster in person. You may start your own *keikokai* by contacting Otsuka Sensei and following his instructions.

Spanish *Keikokai*

Here are a few of the suggested guidelines for a *keikokai*:

1. A *keikokai* is only an informal training group with a group leader. If it works well and follows the instruction of Otsuka Sensei, it may become a true branch dojo in a few years. If it does not follow instruction, it will be officially dissolved by the Meifu Shinkage Ryu *hombu*.
2. Training in a *keikokai* does not earn you rank. Rank can only be awarded to people who have applied for membership in Japan and it is only given by Otsuka Sensei personally.
3. All members of the *keikokai* must share the costs and burdens of training equally.
4. Updates in the form of training photos, videos and personal correspondence with Otsuka Sensei will be required on a regular basis.
5. The *keikokai* will be required to purchase their shuriken from the Meifu Shinkage Ryu *hombu* or their local Meifu Shinkage Ryu instructor. (This is not merely a financial consideration; it is a form of respect in Japanese Budo.)*
6. At least one member of each *keikokai* will be required to train at the Meifu Shinkage Ryu *hombu* in Japan each year.

- The Soke (grandmaster) of a budo school is usually endowed with the copyright for the weapons unique to that school. Technically, it is a tort to manufacture said weapons without the express permission of the Soke. Of course, international laws don't really address this, so people in other countries can do whatever they want. If one wishes to remain in the good graces of a Japanese budo school, however, these rules need to be respected. If, however, ordering from Japan is not possible, then buying from another shuriken maker is acceptable.

If you wish to learn shuriken-jutsu from a qualified instructor, then start saving your money for an airplane ticket to Tokyo and send Otsuka Sensei an e-mail. That might sound like a tall order, but it is much easier than you imagine and it will give you more than enough to work on until you can return for another week or two of lessons.

Embu at Katori shrine.

Members of the public are welcome to attend as long as they email or call Otsuka Sensei in advance and get permission. Otsuka Sensei speaks English very well, so don't be afraid to speak or write to him in English. If you wish to write to him in Japanese, please do so. It will please him to see you making an effort to speak his language. That being said, budo is learned by watching and feeling physical movement, so fluency in Japanese is not required.

There are two Meifu Shinkage Ryu websites, one in English and one in Japanese, that provide a training schedule, maps to the dojo and contact information. They also provide a brief introduction to the art. Those interested in visiting should feel free to contact us through the Meifu Shinkage Ryu Research Group homepage: http://www.geocities.jp/meifuenglish/1p.html

Members of the Meifu Shinkage Ryu and visitors.

Many people want to know where they can buy a set of genuine shuriken for training. Luckily, several of the MSR students are also craftsmen who make blades for us to use. They can be purchased through Otsuka Sensei, but he doesn't sell them to just anybody. He wants to know that the people who buy them are budo students and responsible adults. Shinada San, an experienced student, makes many kinds of shuriken that are almost impossible to find anywhere else. He uses his movie prop-making skills to create an array of well-made shuriken and other budo weapons. Noda San is also an excellent maker of shuriken. There are also shuriken makers in other countries. Be careful when buying blades. Don't waste your money on chrome-plated toys!

Not all shuriken makers are always up and running. You need to take your time and ask questions. If you do buy shuriken from someone, check the dimensions, check the weight. If it is not the proper size and weight, then throwing it will only hurt your development and it may cause you injury or property damage. These are ballistic weapons; think of them as ammunition for a firearm. They need to be the correct caliber or bad things will happen.

Handmade blades of all types on a bench.

Shinada-san working on making shuriken blades.

Acknowledgments

I would like to express my sincere gratitude to the many fine men and women who helped me learn and write about this fascinating art. I have been somewhat obsessed with shuriken since I was 10 years old, but I never really knew anything about it until I went to Japan. Once I reached Japan, there were many generous and talented masters, students and scholars who were very helpful and supportive of this work.

This acknowledgement is in no way complete, and I hope anyone whose name I forgot will forgive me. I am grateful to every one of them.

Brian Alexakis, USA
Daniel Bowley, Australia
Dean Eichler, USA
Dexter Benn, USA
Hatsumi Sensei, Japan
Jason Roybal, USA
Jason Wotherspoon, Australia
Mark Lithgow, Japan
Markk Bush, USA
Nagato Sensei, Japan
Otsuka Sensei, Japan
Paul Richardson, UK
Shea Johnson, USA
Shinada Sensei, Japan
Sleiman Azizi, Japan

I wish to dedicate this book to my daughter, Jessica (Kiyo Nishiyama 西山貴代). I know someday we will meet again.